rockschool®

Guitar
Companion Guide

Multiple examples of the 'unseen tests' in Rockschool exams for practice and improved exam performance

Acknowledgements

Published by Rockschool Ltd. © 2012
Catalogue Number RSK111201
ISBN: 978-1-908920-28-7

AUDIO
Recorded, mixed and mastered at Langlei Studios by Duncan Jordan
Producer: James Uings

MUSICIANS
Stuart Clayton, Fergus Gerrand, Noam Lederman, Stuart Ryan, Ross Stanley

PUBLISHING
Music engraving and book layout by Simon Troup and Jennie Troup of Digital Music Art
Proof and copy editing by Stephen Lawson, Simon Pitt, James Uings and Chris Bird
Cover design by Philip Millard
Cover photography by Adam Gasson

SYLLABUS
Syllabus director: Jeremy Ward
Instrumental specialists: Stuart Clayton, Noam Lederman and James Uings

SPONSORSHIP
Noam Lederman plays Mapex Drums, PAISTE cymbals and uses Vic Firth Sticks
Rockschool would like to thank the following companies for donating instruments used in the cover artwork

PRINTING
Printed and bound in the United Kingdom by Caligraving Ltd
CDs manufactured in the European Union by Software Logistics

DISTRIBUTION
Exclusive Distributors: Music Sales Ltd

CONTACTING ROCKSCHOOL
www.rockschool.co.uk
Telephone: +44 (0)845 460 4747
Fax: +44 (0)845 460 1960

Table of Contents

Welcome to the Rockschool Guitar *Companion Guide*

This book is designed to give teachers, learners and candidates multiple examples of the 'unseen' tests that are to be found within each Rockschool grade exam at Debut and Grades 1–8. The *Companion Guide* contains between three and six examples of each of the following tests:

- Sight Reading (Debut–Grade 5)
- Improvisation & Interpretation (Grades 1–5)*
- Ear Tests (Debut–Grade 8)*
- Quick Study Pieces (Grades 6–8)*
- General Musicianship Questions (Debut–Grade 8)

All of the test examples marked (*) can be found on the audio CDs accompanying this *Companion Guide*. The Quick Study Pieces (QSPs) come in two audio versions: one with a full mix of the QSP and one with the examined instrumental part removed. Please refer to the track listings given in the text.

Teachers, learners and candidates should also refer to the Rockschool *Syllabus Guide* for Guitar where you will find the technical specifications for each section of the exam syllabus, including those parts of the exam (the performance pieces and the Technical Exercises) not covered by this *Companion Guide*. The Guitar *Syllabus Guide* can be found on our website: *www.rockschool.co.uk*. References to the relevant sections of the *Syllabus Guide* can be found in each section of this book.

The purpose of the *Companion Guide* is to give candidates practice examples of the kinds of 'unseen' tests encountered in the grade exam.

If you have any queries about the syllabus for Guitar (or any other exam syllabus offered by Rockschool), please do not hesitate to call us on 0845 460 4747 or email us at *info@rockschool.co.uk*.

The Rockschool website, *www.rockschool.co.uk*, has detailed information on all aspects of our examinations, including examination regulations, detailed marking schemes and marking criteria.

Guitar Notation Explained

THE MUSICAL STAVE shows pitches and rhythms and is divided by lines into bars. Pitches are named after the first seven letters of the alphabet.

TABLATURE graphically represents the guitar fingerboard. Each horizontal line represents a string and each number represents a fret.

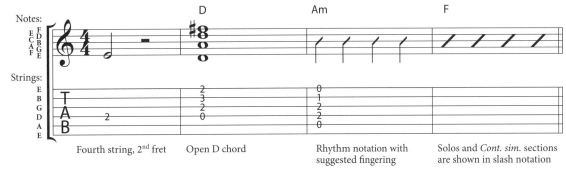

Fourth string, 2nd fret   Open D chord   Rhythm notation with suggested fingering   Solos and *Cont. sim.* sections are shown in slash notation

Definitions For Special Guitar Notation

HAMMER-ON: Pick the lower note, then sound the higher note by fretting it without picking.

PULL-OFF: Pick the higher note then sound the lower note by lifting the finger without picking.

SLIDE: Pick the first note and slide to the next. If the line connects (as below) the second note is *not* repicked.

GLISSANDO: Slide off of a note at the end of its rhythmic value. The note that follows *is* repicked.

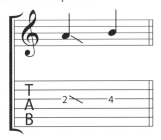

STRING BENDS: Pick the first note then bend (or release the bend) to the pitch indicated in brackets.

VIBRATO: Vibrate the note by bending and releasing the string smoothly and continuously.

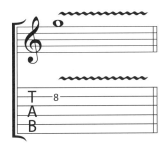

TRILL: Rapidly alternate between the two bracketed notes by hammering on and pulling off.

NATURAL HARMONICS: Lightly touch the string above the indicated fret then pick to sound a harmonic.

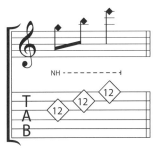

PINCHED HARMONICS: Bring the thumb of the picking hand into contact with the string immediately after the pick.

PICK-HAND TAP: Strike the indicated note with a finger from the picking hand. Usually followed by a pull-off.

FRET-HAND TAP: As pick-hand tap, but use fretting hand. Usually followed by a pull-off or hammer-on.

QUARTER-TONE BEND: Pick the note indicated and bend the string up by a quarter tone.

PRE-BENDS: Before picking the note, bend the string from the fret indicated between the staves, to the equivalent pitch indicated in brackets in the TAB.

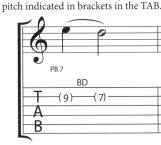

WHAMMY BAR BEND: Use the whammy bar to bend notes to the pitches indicated in brackets in the TAB.

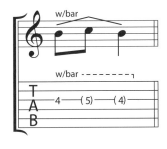

D.%. al Coda

D.C. al Fine

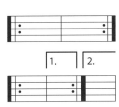

- Go back to the sign (%), then play until the bar marked To Coda ⊕ then skip to the section marked ⊕ Coda.

- Go back to the beginning of the song and play until the bar marked Fine (end).

- Repeat bars between signs.

- When a repeated section has different endings, play the first ending only the first time and the second ending only the second time.

Sight Reading Debut

Candidates attempting a Debut grade exam are required to take a Sight Reading test. Candidates attempting Grades 1–5 inclusive have a choice of taking **either** the Sight Reading **or** the Improvisation & Interpretation test in the exam. Six examples of the types of Sight Reading tests required in the exam are shown below in grade order. A summary of the technical specifications of each test offered to candidates in the exam can be found in the Guitar *Syllabus Guide* in the summary table on page 32. The *Syllabus Guide* can be found on the Rockschool website: *www.rockschool.co.uk*. Please note that in Grades 4 and 5 each Sight Reading test also includes two bars of improvisation.

You will be asked to prepare a Sight Reading test which is given to you by the examiner. The examiner will allow you 90 seconds to prepare the test and will set the tempo for you on a metronome. You can choose to play with or without the metronome. TAB fingerings are given along with standard notation in all Sight Reading tests at all grades. The examiner will offer you the metronome, which can be used during your practice time or as a four-beat indication of the tempo. Choose which works best for you. It is best to stick with the method you have used while preparing at home for the exam. The examiner will also offer you the metronome for your performance.

Debut
The following examples are indicative of the types of test you will be given in the Debut exam.

Example 1

♩=70

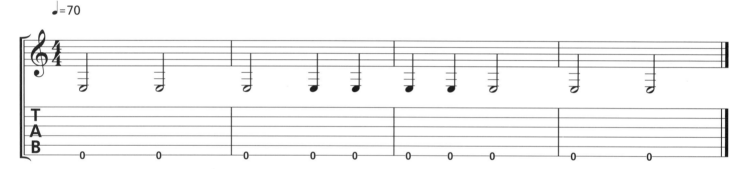

Example 2

♩=70

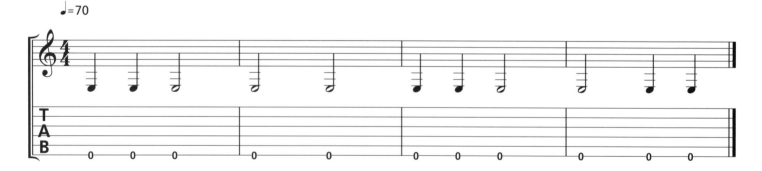

Example 3

♩=70

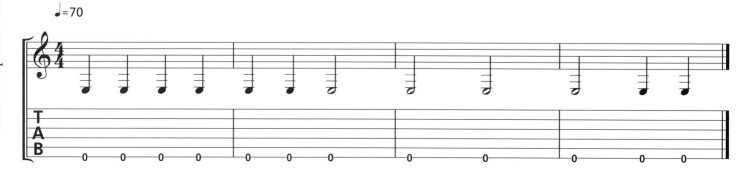

Example 4

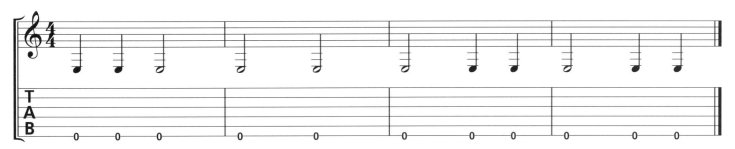

Example 5

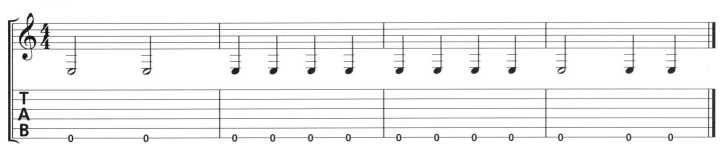

Example 6

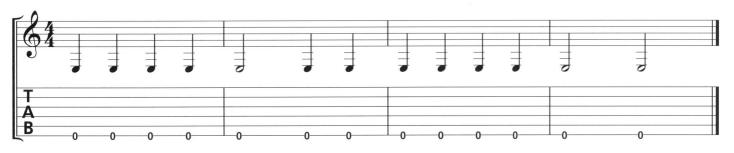

Sight Reading Grade 1

Grade 1

The following examples are indicative of the types of test you will be given in the Grade 1 exam.

Example 1

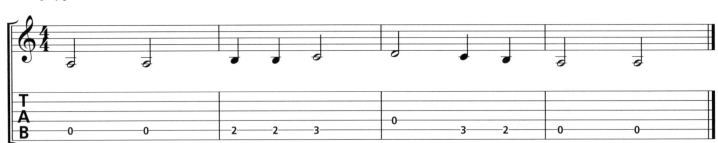

Example 2

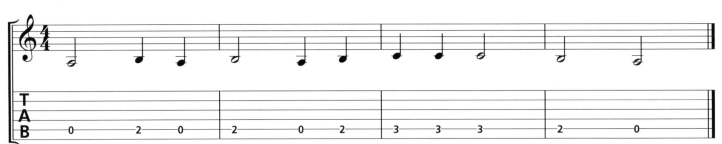

Example 3

Example 4

♩=70

Example 5

♩=70

Example 6

♩=70

Sight Reading Grade 2

Grade 2

The following examples are indicative of the types of test you will be given in the Grade 2 exam.

Example 1

Example 2

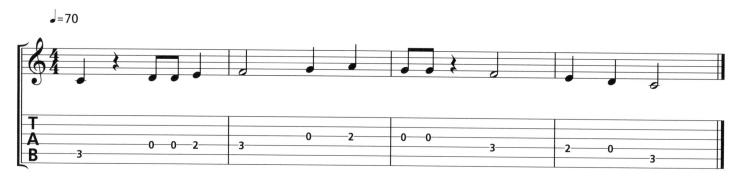

Example 3

Example 4

Example 5

Example 6

Grade 3

The following examples are indicative of the types of test you will be given in the Grade 3 exam.

Example 1

Example 2

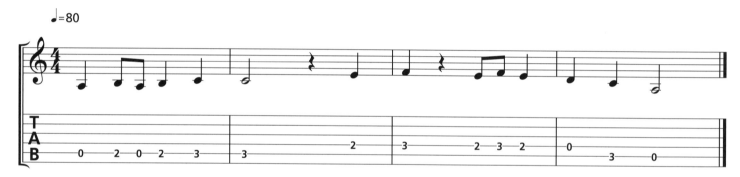

Example 3

Example 4

♩=80

Example 5

♩=80

Example 6

♩=80

Sight Reading Grade 4

Grade 4

The following examples are indicative of the types of test you will be given in the Grade 4 exam. Please note that in Grade 4 the Sight Reading tests contain a small amount of improvisation and interpretation. This consists of a two-bar section to be found at the end of each test.

Example 1

Example 2

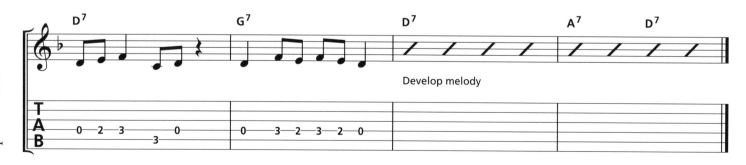

Example 3

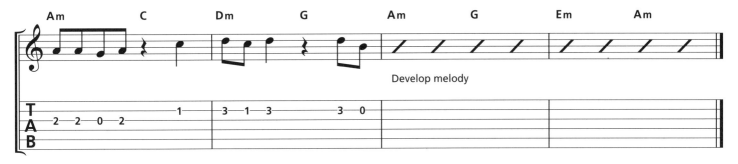

Develop melody

Example 4

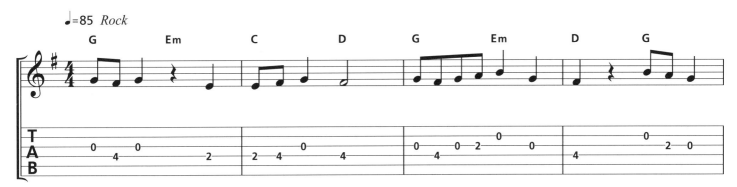

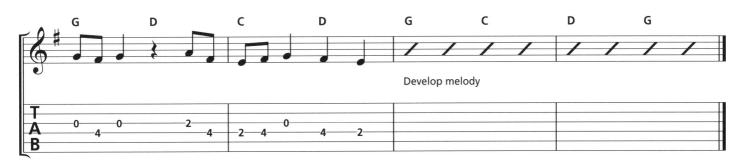

Develop melody

Example 5

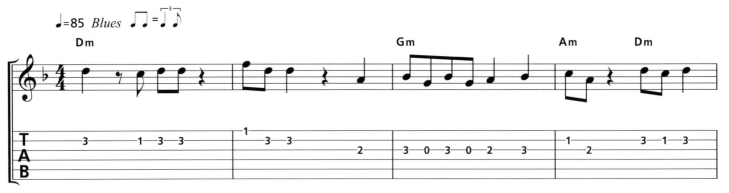

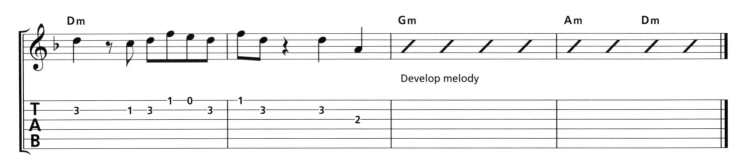

Develop melody

Example 6

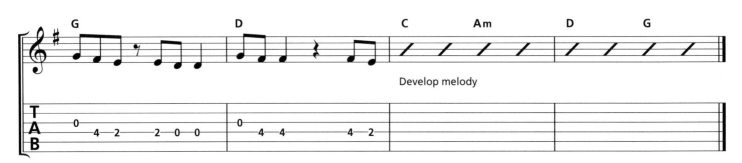

Develop melody

rockschool®

Guitar
Companion Guide

Multiple examples of the 'unseen tests' in Rockschool exams for practice and improved exam performance

Acknowledgements

Published by Rockschool Ltd. © 2012
Catalogue Number RSK111201
ISBN: 978-1-908920-28-7

AUDIO
Recorded, mixed and mastered at Langlei Studios by Duncan Jordan
Producer: James Uings

MUSICIANS
Stuart Clayton, Fergus Gerrand, Noam Lederman, Stuart Ryan, Ross Stanley

PUBLISHING
Music engraving and book layout by Simon Troup and Jennie Troup of Digital Music Art
Proof and copy editing by Stephen Lawson, Simon Pitt, James Uings and Chris Bird
Cover design by Philip Millard
Cover photography by Adam Gasson

SYLLABUS
Syllabus director: Jeremy Ward
Instrumental specialists: Stuart Clayton, Noam Lederman and James Uings

SPONSORSHIP
Noam Lederman plays Mapex Drums, PAISTE cymbals and uses Vic Firth Sticks
Rockschool would like to thank the following companies for donating instruments used in the cover artwork

PRINTING
Printed and bound in the United Kingdom by Caligraving Ltd
CDs manufactured in the European Union by Software Logistics

DISTRIBUTION
Exclusive Distributors: Music Sales Ltd

CONTACTING ROCKSCHOOL
www.rockschool.co.uk
Telephone: +44 (0)845 460 4747
Fax: +44 (0)845 460 1960

Table of Contents

Introductions & Information

Sections

Welcome to the Rockschool Guitar *Companion Guide*

This book is designed to give teachers, learners and candidates multiple examples of the 'unseen' tests that are to be found within each Rockschool grade exam at Debut and Grades 1–8. The *Companion Guide* contains between three and six examples of each of the following tests:

- Sight Reading (Debut–Grade 5)
- Improvisation & Interpretation (Grades 1–5)*
- Ear Tests (Debut–Grade 8)*
- Quick Study Pieces (Grades 6–8)*
- General Musicianship Questions (Debut–Grade 8)

All of the test examples marked (*) can be found on the audio CDs accompanying this *Companion Guide*. The Quick Study Pieces (QSPs) come in two audio versions: one with a full mix of the QSP and one with the examined instrumental part removed. Please refer to the track listings given in the text.

Teachers, learners and candidates should also refer to the Rockschool *Syllabus Guide* for Guitar where you will find the technical specifications for each section of the exam syllabus, including those parts of the exam (the performance pieces and the Technical Exercises) not covered by this *Companion Guide*. The Guitar *Syllabus Guide* can be found on our website: *www.rockschool.co.uk*. References to the relevant sections of the *Syllabus Guide* can be found in each section of this book.

The purpose of the *Companion Guide* is to give candidates practice examples of the kinds of 'unseen' tests encountered in the grade exam.

If you have any queries about the syllabus for Guitar (or any other exam syllabus offered by Rockschool), please do not hesitate to call us on 0845 460 4747 or email us at *info@rockschool.co.uk*.

The Rockschool website, *www.rockschool.co.uk*, has detailed information on all aspects of our examinations, including examination regulations, detailed marking schemes and marking criteria.

Guitar Notation Explained

THE MUSICAL STAVE shows pitches and rhythms and is divided by lines into bars. Pitches are named after the first seven letters of the alphabet.

TABLATURE graphically represents the guitar fingerboard. Each horizontal line represents a string and each number represents a fret.

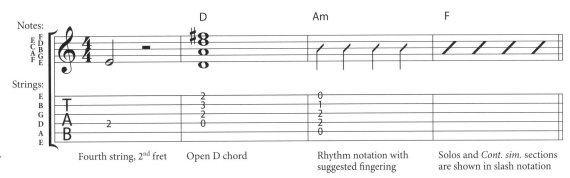

Fourth string, 2nd fret   Open D chord   Rhythm notation with suggested fingering   Solos and *Cont. sim.* sections are shown in slash notation

Definitions For Special Guitar Notation

HAMMER-ON: Pick the lower note, then sound the higher note by fretting it without picking.

PULL-OFF: Pick the higher note then sound the lower note by lifting the finger without picking.

SLIDE: Pick the first note and slide to the next. If the line connects (as below) the second note is *not* repicked.

GLISSANDO: Slide off of a note at the end of its rhythmic value. The note that follows *is* repicked.

STRING BENDS: Pick the first note then bend (or release the bend) to the pitch indicated in brackets.

VIBRATO: Vibrate the note by bending and releasing the string smoothly and continuously.

TRILL: Rapidly alternate between the two bracketed notes by hammering on and pulling off.

NATURAL HARMONICS: Lightly touch the string above the indicated fret then pick to sound a harmonic.

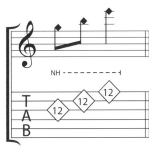

PINCHED HARMONICS: Bring the thumb of the picking hand into contact with the string immediately after the pick.

PICK-HAND TAP: Strike the indicated note with a finger from the picking hand. Usually followed by a pull-off.

FRET-HAND TAP: As pick-hand tap, but use fretting hand. Usually followed by a pull-off or hammer-on.

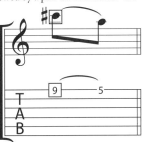

QUARTER-TONE BEND: Pick the note indicated and bend the string up by a quarter tone.

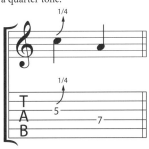

PRE-BENDS: Before picking the note, bend the string from the fret indicated between the staves, to the equivalent pitch indicated in brackets in the TAB.

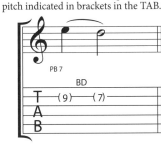

WHAMMY BAR BEND: Use the whammy bar to bend notes to the pitches indicated in brackets in the TAB.

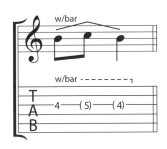

D.%. al Coda

D.C. al Fine

- Go back to the sign (%), then play until the bar marked To Coda ⊕ then skip to the section marked ⊕ Coda.

- Go back to the beginning of the song and play until the bar marked Fine (end).

- Repeat bars between signs.

- When a repeated section has different endings, play the first ending only the first time and the second ending only the second time.

Sight Reading Debut

Candidates attempting a Debut grade exam are required to take a Sight Reading test. Candidates attempting Grades 1–5 inclusive have a choice of taking **either** the Sight Reading **or** the Improvisation & Interpretation test in the exam. Six examples of the types of Sight Reading tests required in the exam are shown below in grade order. A summary of the technical specifications of each test offered to candidates in the exam can be found in the Guitar *Syllabus Guide* in the summary table on page 32. The *Syllabus Guide* can be found on the Rockschool website: *www.rockschool.co.uk*. Please note that in Grades 4 and 5 each Sight Reading test also includes two bars of improvisation.

You will be asked to prepare a Sight Reading test which is given to you by the examiner. The examiner will allow you 90 seconds to prepare the test and will set the tempo for you on a metronome. You can choose to play with or without the metronome. TAB fingerings are given along with standard notation in all Sight Reading tests at all grades. The examiner will offer you the metronome, which can be used during your practice time or as a four-beat indication of the tempo. Choose which works best for you. It is best to stick with the method you have used while preparing at home for the exam. The examiner will also offer you the metronome for your performance.

Debut
The following examples are indicative of the types of test you will be given in the Debut exam.

Example 1

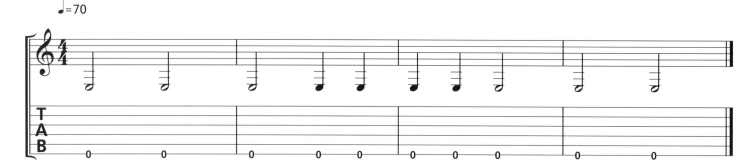

Example 2

Example 3

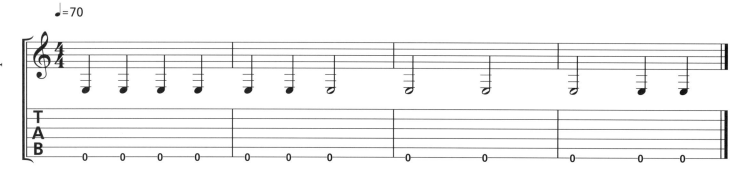

Example 4

♩=70

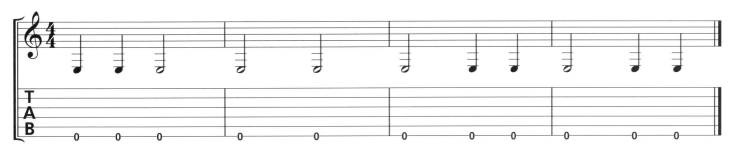

Example 5

♩=70

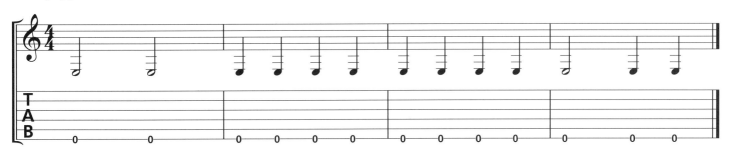

Example 6

♩=70

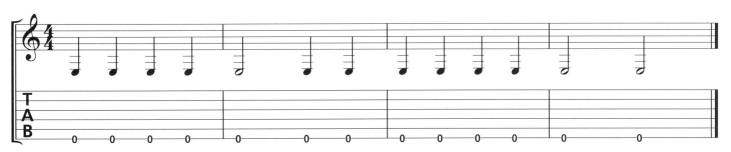

Sight Reading Grade 1

Grade 1

The following examples are indicative of the types of test you will be given in the Grade 1 exam.

Example 1

Example 2

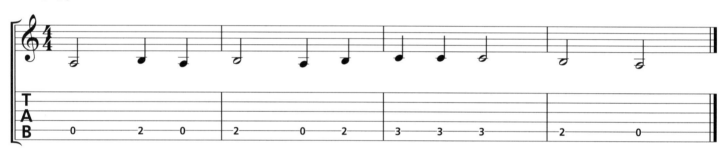

Example 3

Example 4

♩=70

Example 5

♩=70

Example 6

♩=70

Grade 2

The following examples are indicative of the types of test you will be given in the Grade 2 exam.

Example 1

Example 2

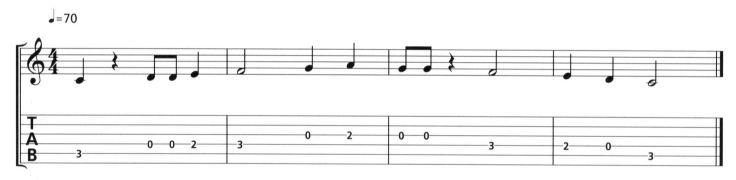

Example 3

Example 4

♩=70

Example 5

♩=70

Example 6

♩=70

Grade 3

The following examples are indicative of the types of test you will be given in the Grade 3 exam.

Example 1

Example 2

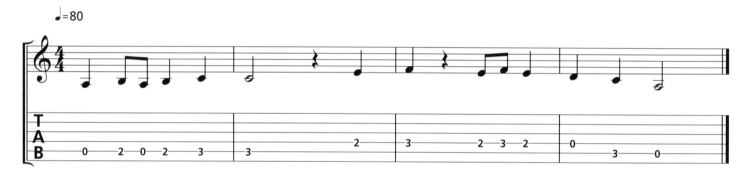

Example 3

Example 4

Example 5

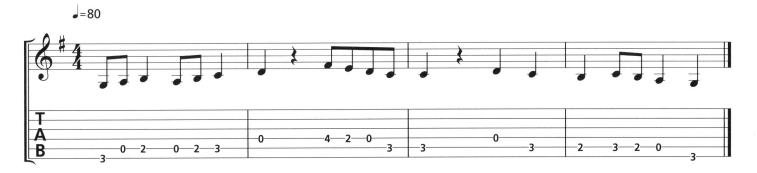

Example 6

Grade 4

The following examples are indicative of the types of test you will be given in the Grade 4 exam. Please note that in Grade 4 the Sight Reading tests contain a small amount of improvisation and interpretation. This consists of a two-bar section to be found at the end of each test.

Example 1

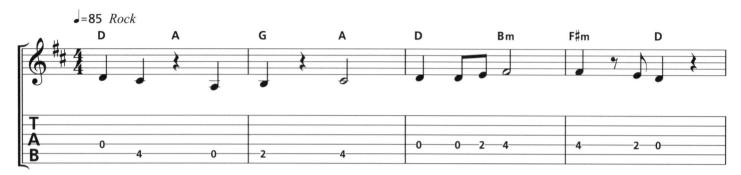

Example 2

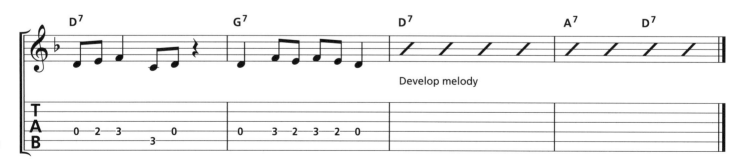

Example 3

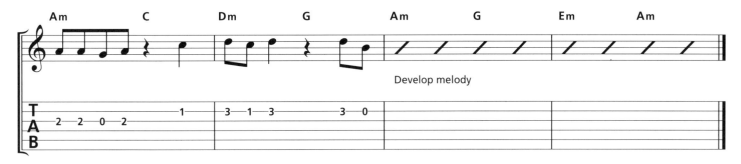

Develop melody

Example 4

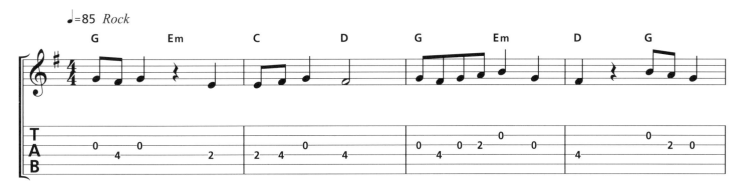

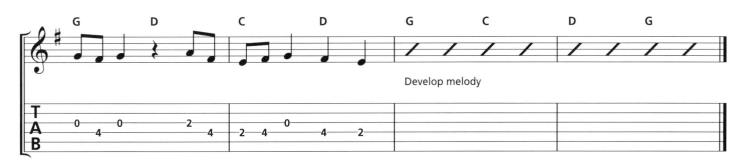

Develop melody

Example 5

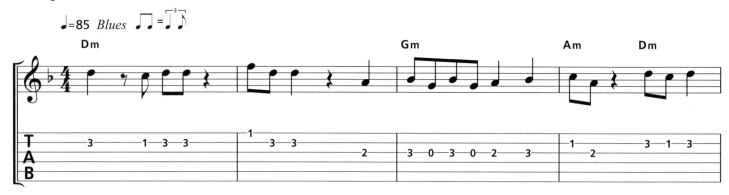

Develop melody

Example 6

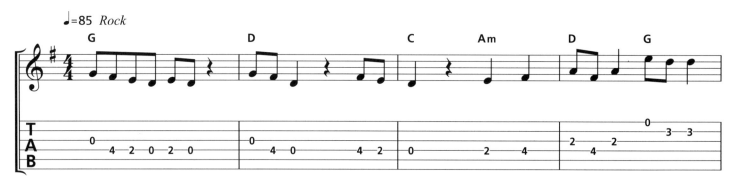

Develop melody

Example 3

CD 1 Tracks 59 & 60

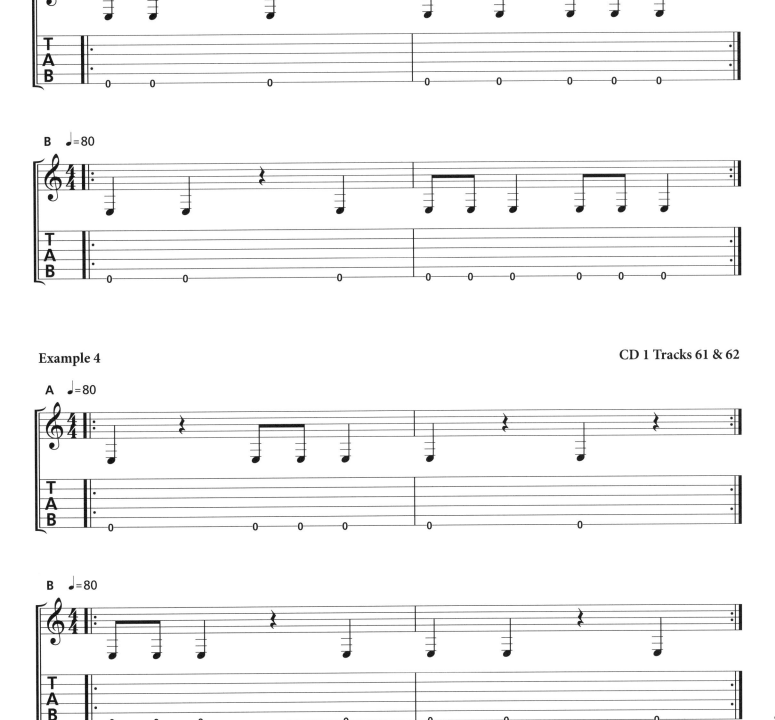

Example 4

CD 1 Tracks 61 & 62

Example 5

CD 1 Tracks 63 & 64

Example 6

CD 1 Tracks 65 & 66

Grade 1 Test 1: Melodic Recall

The examiner will play you three notes in sequence. You will identify whether the notes are higher or lower (up or down) in sequence. You will hear the test twice. Each time the test is played it is preceded by a one-bar vocal count-in.

Candidate may answer either: "higher/lower" or "up/down".

Example 1   CD 1 Track 67

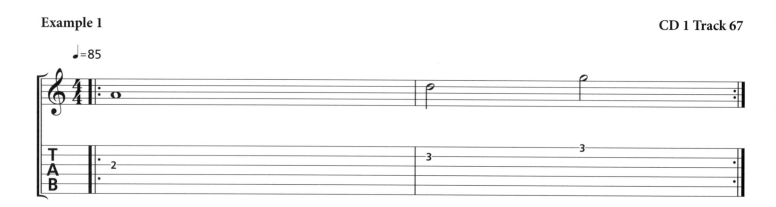

Example 2   CD 1 Track 68

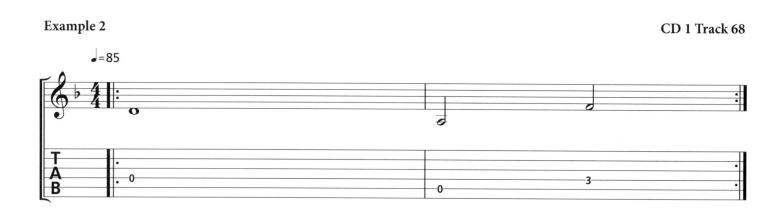

Example 3   CD 1 Track 69

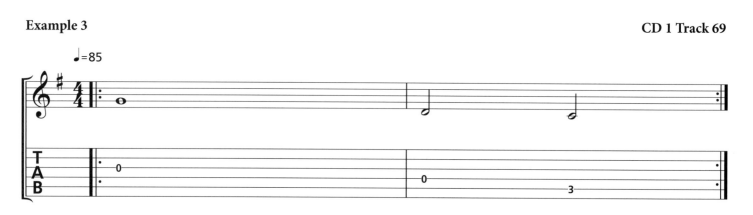

Example 4 CD 1 Track 70

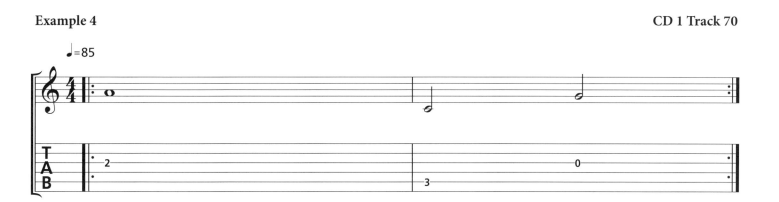

Example 5 CD 1 Track 71

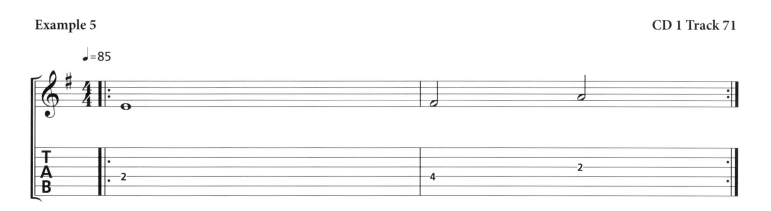

Example 6 CD 1 Track 72

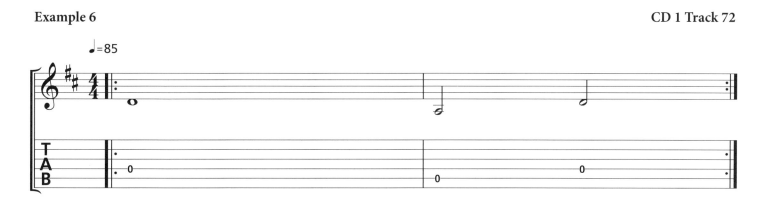

Grade 1 Test 2: Rhythmic Recall

The examiner will play you a two-bar rhythm played to a drum backing on the lowest-sounding E string. You will hear the test twice. You will be asked to play the rhythm back. You will then be asked to identify the rhythm from two printed examples shown to you. Each time the test is played it is preceded by a one-bar count-in. There will be a short gap for you to practise. Next you will hear a *vocal* count-in and you will then play the rhythm to the drum backing.

Example 1   **CD 1 Tracks 73 & 74**

Example 2   **CD 1 Tracks 75 & 76**

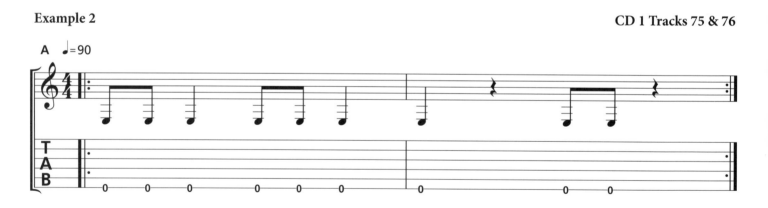

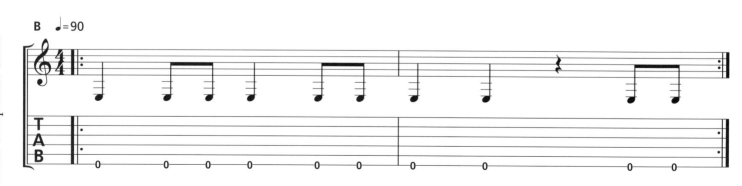

Example 3

CD 1 Tracks 77 & 78

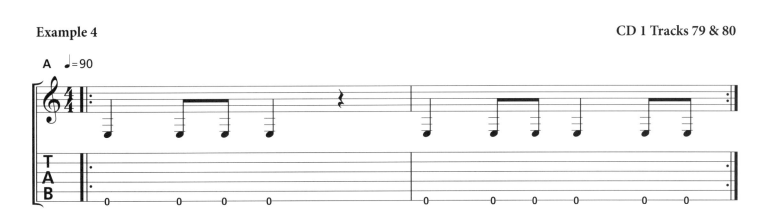

Example 4

CD 1 Tracks 79 & 80

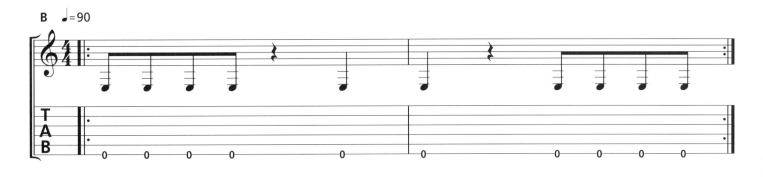

Example 5

CD 1 Tracks 81 & 82

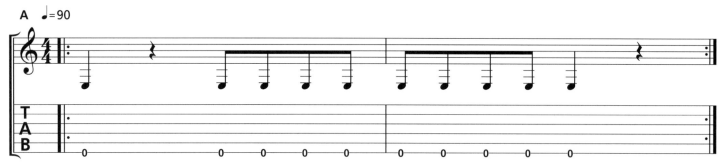

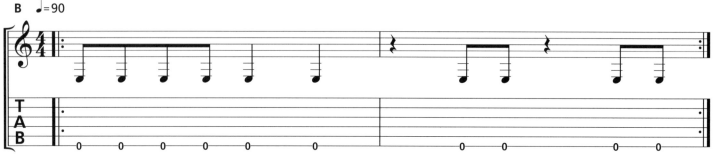

Example 6

CD 1 Tracks 83 & 84

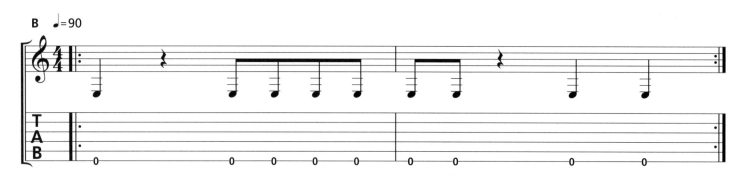

Grade 2 Test 1: Melodic Recall

The examiner will play you a two-bar melody with a drum backing using the C minor pentatonic scale. The first note of the melody will be the root note and the first interval will be ascending. You will play the melody back on your instrument. You will hear the test twice. Each time the test is played it is preceded by a one-bar count-in. There will be a short gap for you to practise. Next you will hear a *vocal* count-in and you will then play the melody to the drum backing.

Example 1

CD 2 Track 1

Example 2

CD 2 Track 2

Example 3

CD 2 Track 3

Example 4

CD 2 Track 4

Example 5

CD 2 Track 5

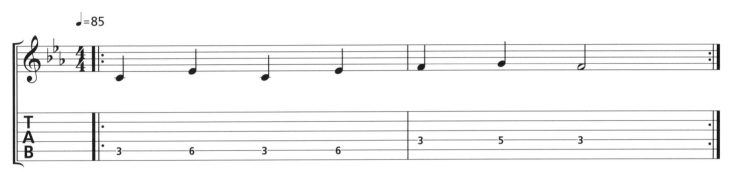

Example 6

CD 2 Track 6

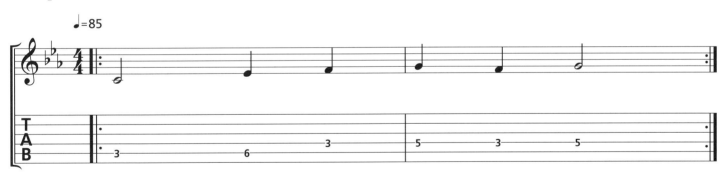

Grade 2 Test 2: Rhythmic Recall

The examiner will play you a two-bar rhythm played to a drum backing on the lowest-sounding E string. You will hear the test twice. You will be asked to play the rhythm back. You will then be asked to identify the rhythm from two printed examples shown to you. Each time the test is played it is preceded by a one-bar count-in. There will be a short gap for you to practise. Next you will hear a *vocal* count-in and you will then play the rhythm to the drum backing.

Example 1 CD 2 Tracks 7 & 8

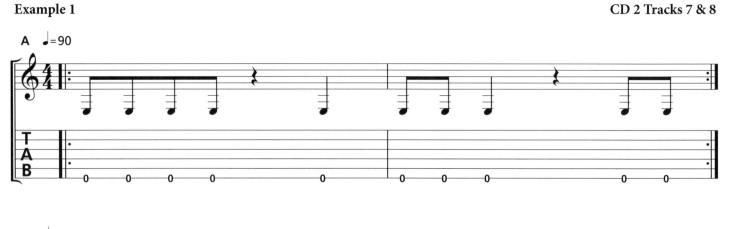

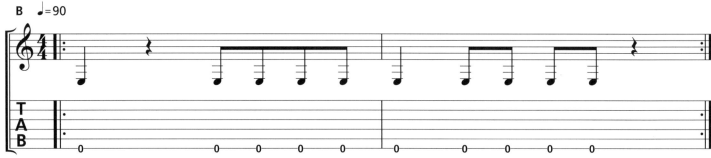

Example 2 CD 2 Tracks 9 & 10

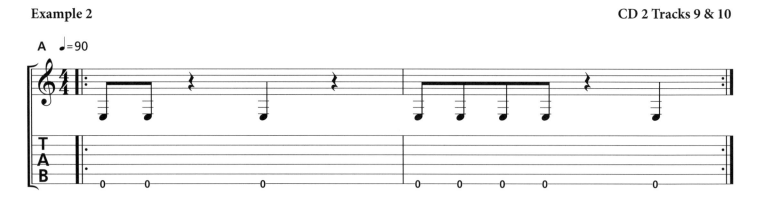

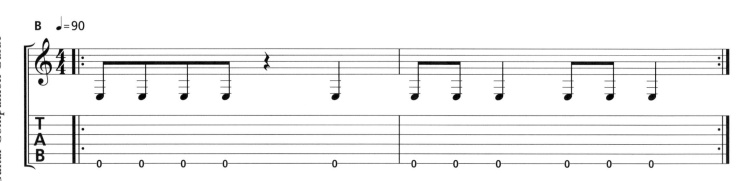

Example 3

CD 2 Tracks 11 & 12

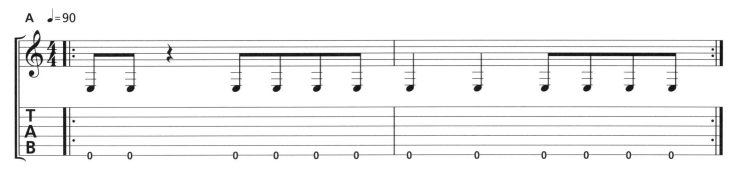

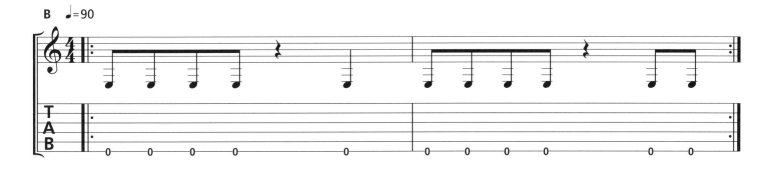

Example 4

CD 2 Tracks 13 & 14

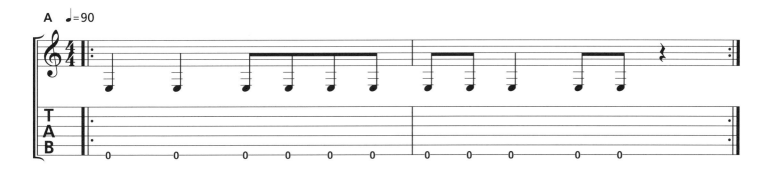

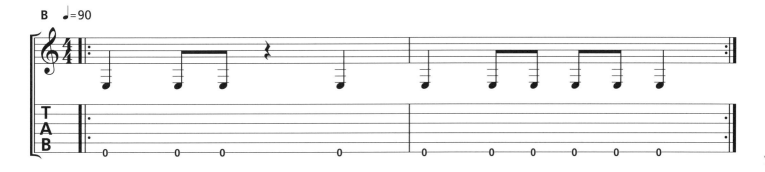

Example 5

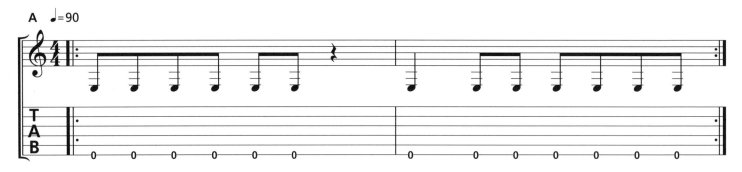

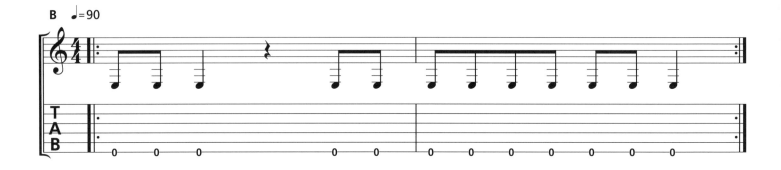

Example 6

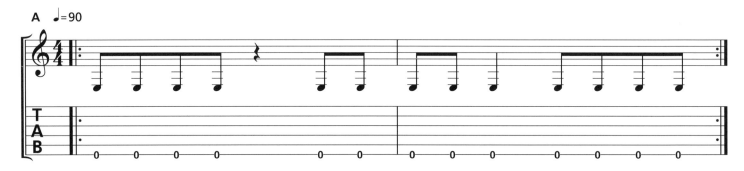

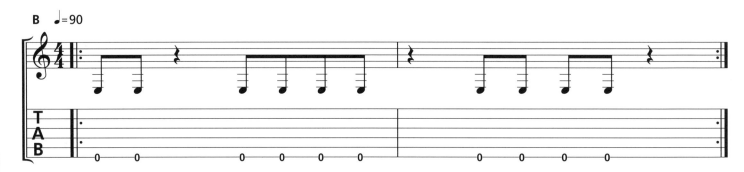

Grade 3 Test 1: Melodic Recall

The examiner will play you a two-bar melody with a drum backing using the G minor pentatonic scale. The first note of the melody will be the root note and the first interval will be ascending. You will play the melody back on your instrument. You will hear the test twice. Each time the test is played it is preceded by a one-bar count-in. There will be a short gap for you to practise after you have heard the test for the second time. Next you will hear a *vocal* count-in and you will then play the melody to the drum backing.

Example 1   CD 2 Track 19

Example 2   CD 2 Track 20

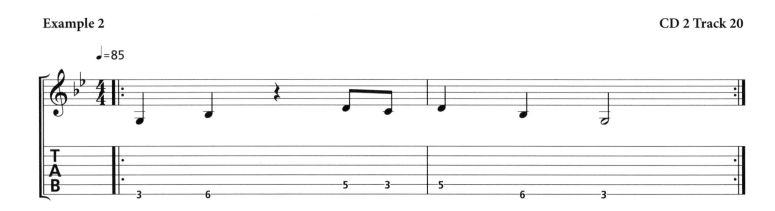

Example 3   CD 2 Track 21

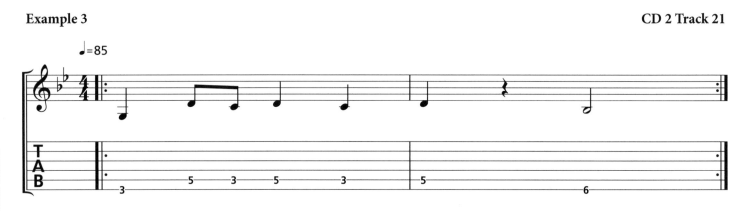

Example 4

CD 2 Track 22

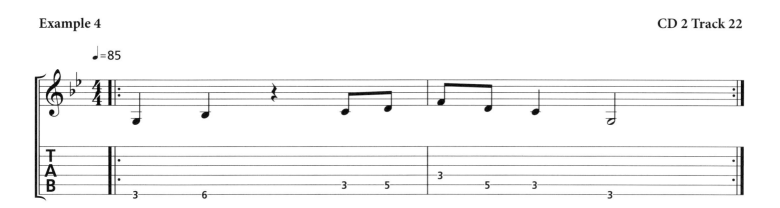

Example 5

CD 2 Track 23

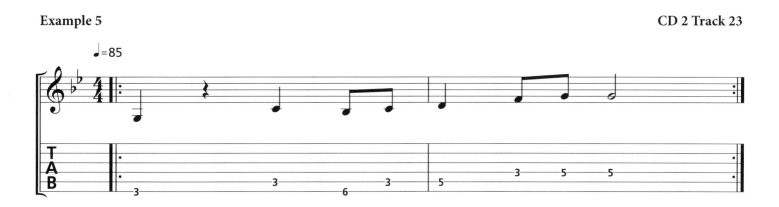

Example 6

CD 2 Track 24

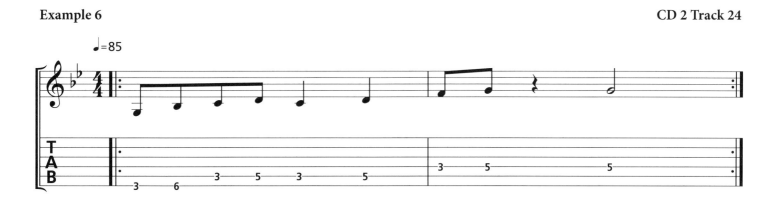

Grade 3 Test 2: Rhythmic Recall
The examiner will play you a two-bar rhythm played to a drum backing on the lowest-sounding E string. You will hear the test twice. You will be asked to play the rhythm back. You will then be asked to identify the rhythm from two printed examples shown to you. Each time the test is played it is preceded by a one-bar count-in. There will be a short gap for you to practise. Next you will hear a *vocal* count-in and you will then play the rhythm to the drum backing.

Example 1　　　　　　　　　　　　　　**CD 2 Tracks 25 & 26**

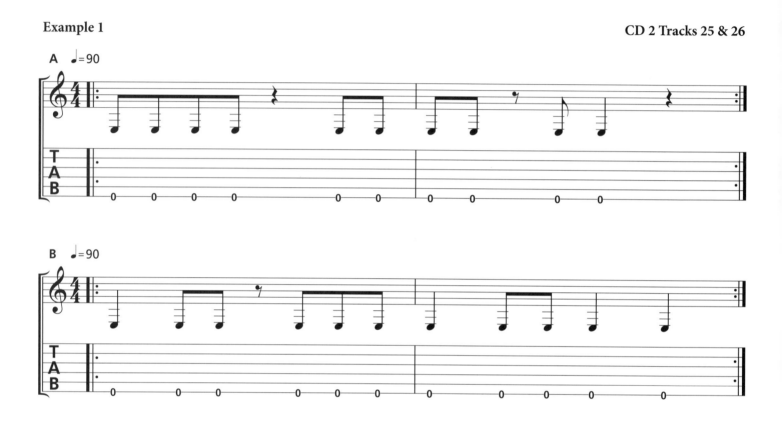

Example 2　　　　　　　　　　　　　　**CD 2 Tracks 27 & 28**

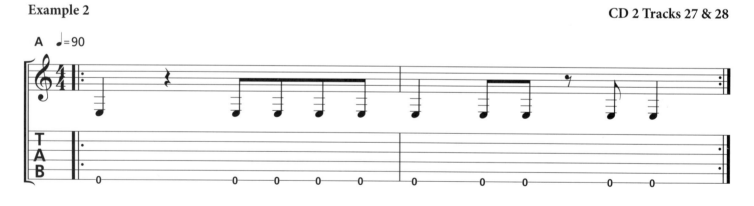

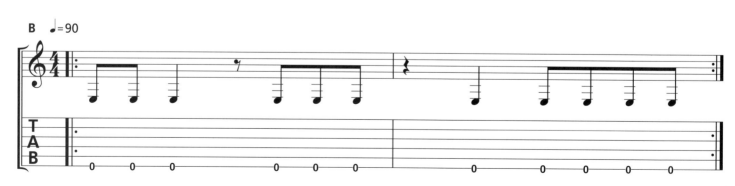

Example 3

CD 2 Tracks 29 & 30

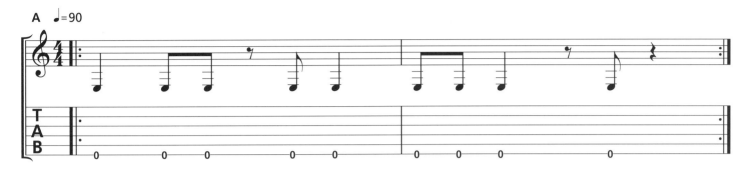

Example 4

CD 2 Tracks 31 & 32

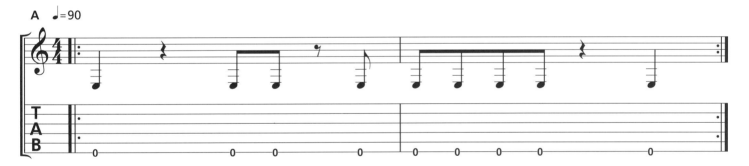

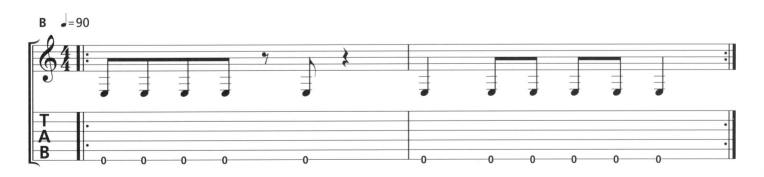

Example 5

CD 2 Tracks 33 & 34

Example 6

CD 2 Tracks 35 & 36

Grade 4 Test 1: Melodic Recall

The examiner will play you a two-bar melody with a drum backing using either the C major pentatonic or B minor pentatonic scales. The first note of the melody will be the root note and the first interval will be descending. You will play the melody back on your instrument. You will hear the test twice.

Each time the test is played the sequence is: count-in, root note, count-in, melody. There will be a short gap for you to practise after you have heard the test for the second time. You will hear the count-in and root note for the third time followed by a *vocal* count-in and you will then play the melody to the drum backing.

Example 1   **CD 2 Track 37**

Example 2   **CD 2 Track 38**

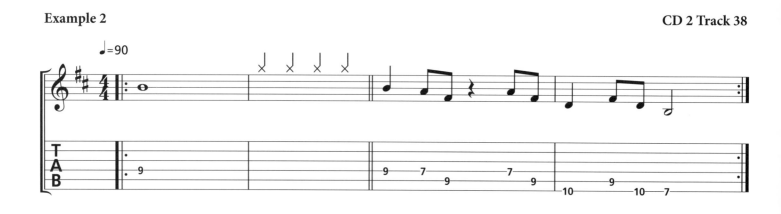

Example 3   **CD 2 Track 39**

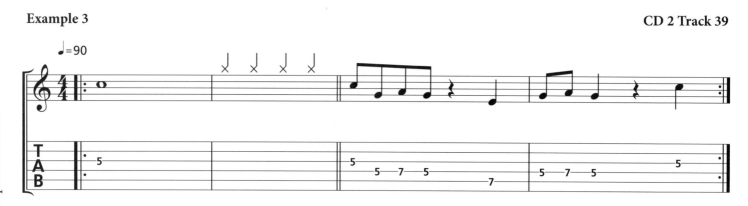

Example 4

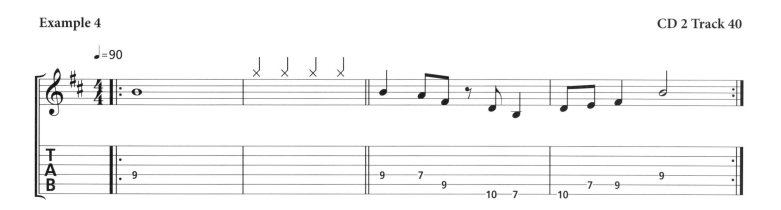

Example 5

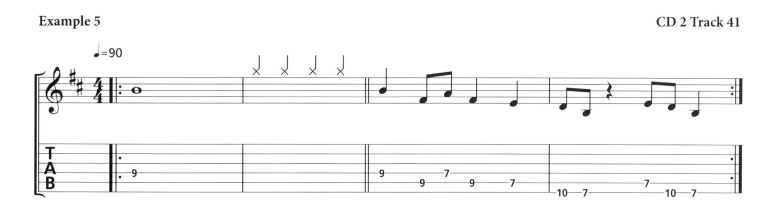

Example 6

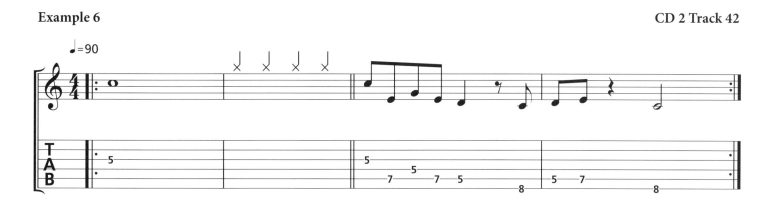

Grade 4 Test 2: Harmonic Recall

The examiner will play you a tonic chord followed by a two-bar chord sequence in the key of C major played to a bass and drum backing. The sequence will be drawn from the I, IV and V chords and may occur in any combination. You will be asked to play the chord sequence to the drum backing in the rhythm shown in the examples below. This rhythm will be used in all examples of this test given in the exam. You will then be asked to identify the sequence you have played to the examiner. You will hear the test twice.

Each time the test is played the sequence is: count-in, tonic, count-in, chords. There will be a short gap for you to practise after you have heard the test for the second time. You will hear the count-in and tonic for the third time followed by a *vocal* count-in then you will play the chords to the drum backing. You should then identify the chords.

Example 1   CD 2 Track 43

Example 2   CD 2 Track 44

Example 3   CD 2 Track 45

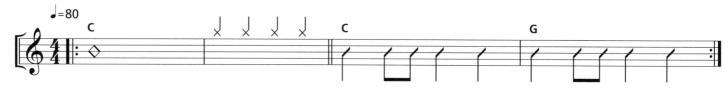

Example 4

CD 2 Track 46

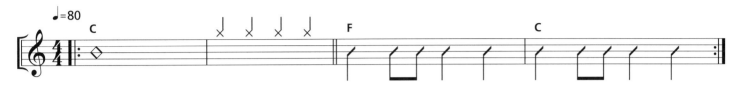

Example 5

CD 2 Track 47

Example 6

CD 2 Track 48

Grade 5 Test 1: Melodic Recall

The examiner will play you a two-bar melody with a drum backing using either the D major pentatonic or A minor pentatonic scale. The first note of the melody will be the root note and the first interval will be descending. You will play the melody back on your instrument. You will hear the test twice.

Each time the test is played the sequence is: count-in, root note, count-in, melody. There will be a short gap for you to practise after you have heard the test for the second time. You will hear the count-in and root note for the third time followed by a *vocal* count-in and you will then play the melody to the drum backing.

Example 1

CD 2 Track 49

Example 2

CD 2 Track 50

Example 3

CD 2 Track 51

Example 4 CD 2 Track 52

Example 5 CD 2 Track 53

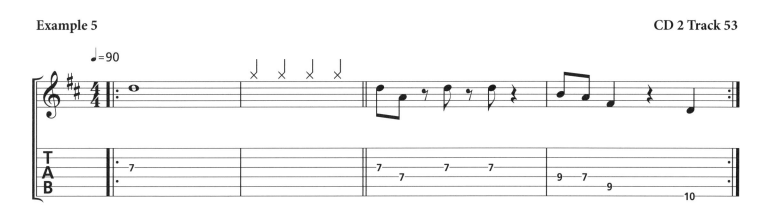

Example 6 CD 2 Track 54

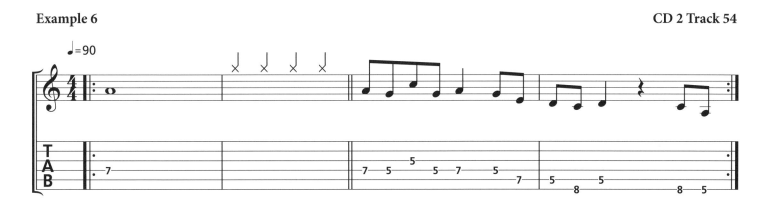

Grade 5 Test 2: Harmonic Recall

The examiner will play you a tonic chord followed by a four-bar chord sequence in the key of G major played to a drum backing. The sequence will be drawn from the I, IV, V and vi chords and may occur in any combination. You will be asked to play the chord sequence to the drum backing in the rhythm shown in the examples below. This rhythm will be used in all examples of this test given in the exam. You will then be asked to identify the sequence you have played to the examiner. You will hear the test twice.

Each time the test is played the sequence is: count-in, tonic, count-in, chords. There will be a short gap for you to practise after you have heard the test for the second time. You will hear the count-in and tonic for the third time followed by a *vocal* count-in then you will play the chords to the drum backing. You should then name the chord sequence, including chord types (i.e. major or minor).

Example 1   CD 2 Track 55

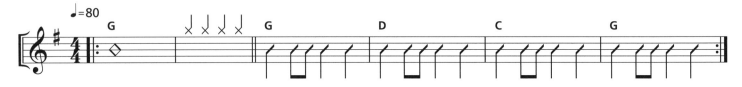

Example 2   CD 2 Track 56

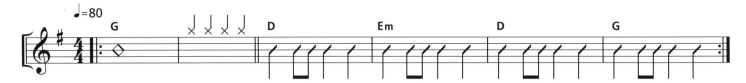

Example 3   CD 2 Track 57

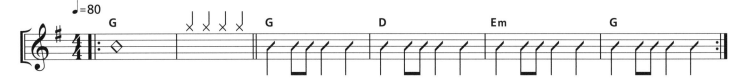

Example 4

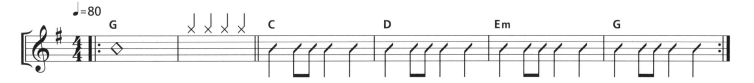

Example 5

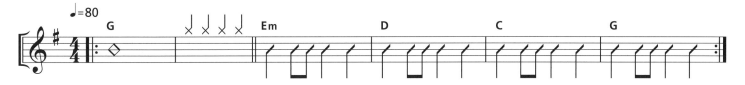

Example 6

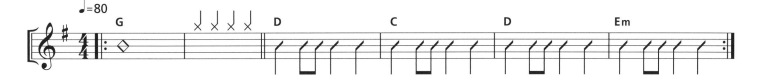

Grade 6 Test 1: Melodic Recall

The examiner will play you a two-bar melody with a bass and drum backing using either the D major pentatonic, D minor pentatonic or G natural minor scale. The first note of the melody will be *either* the root note *or* fifth and the first interval will be *either* ascending *or* descending. You will play the melody back on your instrument. You will hear the test twice.

Each time the test is played the sequence is: count-in, root note, count-in, melody. There will be a short gap for you to practise after you have heard the test for the second time. You will hear the count-in and root note for the third time followed by a *vocal* count-in and you will then play the melody to the bass and drum backing.

Example 1　　　　　　　　　　　　　　　　　　　　　　　　　CD 2 Track 61

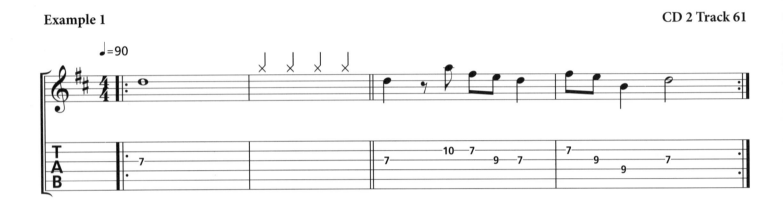

Example 2　　　　　　　　　　　　　　　　　　　　　　　　　CD 2 Track 62

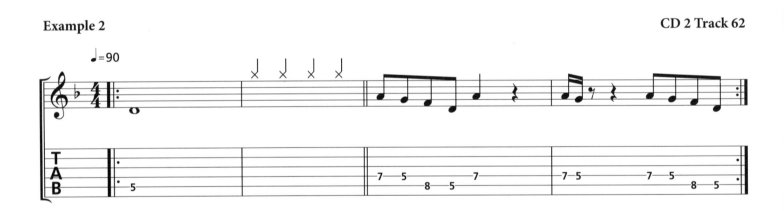

Example 3　　　　　　　　　　　　　　　　　　　　　　　　　CD 2 Track 63

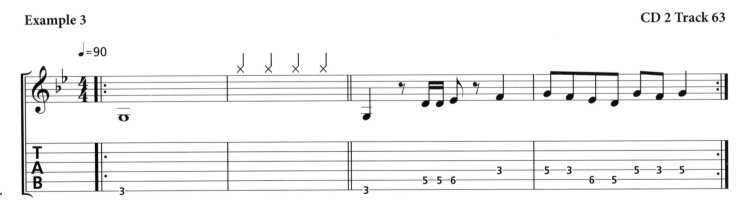

Example 4

CD 2 Track 64

Example 5

CD 2 Track 65

Example 6

CD 2 Track 66

Grade 6 Test 2: Harmonic Recall

The examiner will play you a tonic chord followed by a four-bar chord sequence in the key of D major played to a bass and drum backing. The sequence will use the I, ii, iii, IV, V and vi chords and will incorporate a dominant^7 (V^7) chord. You will be asked to play the chord sequence to the bass and drum backing in the rhythm shown in the examples below. This rhythm will be used in all examples of this test given in the exam. You will then be asked to identify the sequence you have played to the examiner, including any chord extensions. You will hear the test twice.

Each time the test is played the sequence is: count-in, tonic, count-in, chords. There will be a short gap for you to practise after you have heard the test for the second time. You will hear the count-in and tonic for the third time followed by a *vocal* count-in and you will then play the chords to the bass and drum backing. You should then name the chord sequence, including the chord type and any extensions.

Example 1

CD 2 Track 67

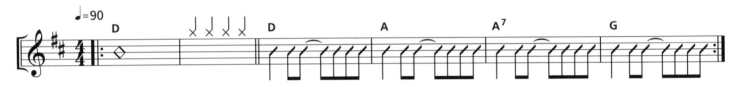

Example 2

CD 2 Track 68

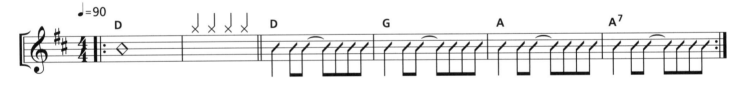

Example 3

CD 2 Track 69

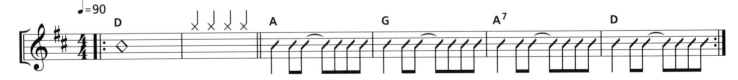

Example 4

CD 2 Track 70

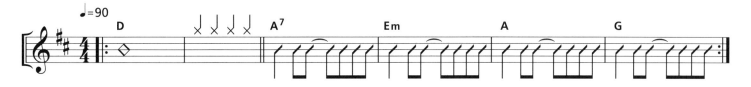

Example 5

CD 2 Track 71

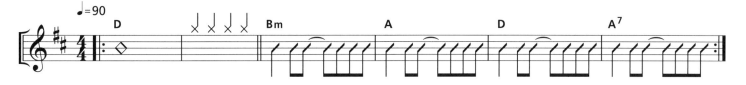

Example 6

CD 2 Track 72

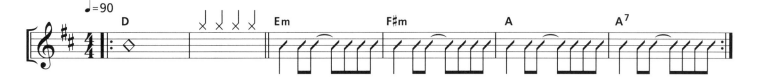

Grade 7 Test 1: Melodic Recall

The examiner will play you a two-bar melody with a bass and drum backing using either the A major pentatonic, C minor pentatonic or A natural minor scale. The first note of the melody will be **either** the root note **or** fifth and the first interval will be **either** ascending **or** descending. You will play the melody back on your instrument. You will hear the test twice.

Each time the test is played the sequence is: count-in, root note, count-in, melody. There will be a short gap for you to practise after you have heard the test for the second time. You will hear the count-in and root note for the third time followed by a *vocal* count-in and you will then play the melody to the bass and drum backing.

Example 1   **CD 2 Track 73**

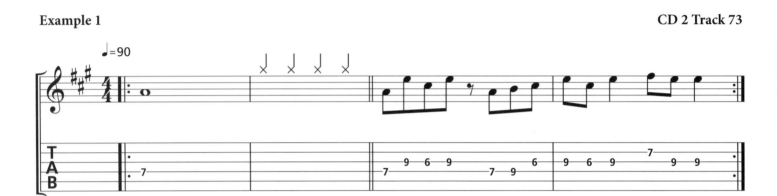

Example 2   **CD 2 Track 74**

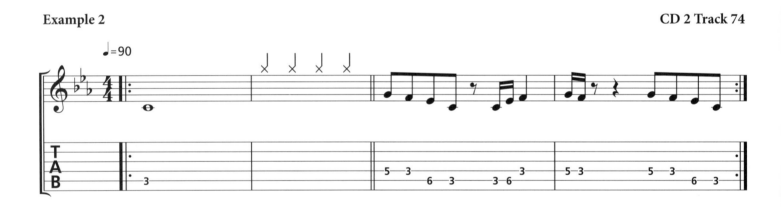

Example 3   **CD 2 Track 75**

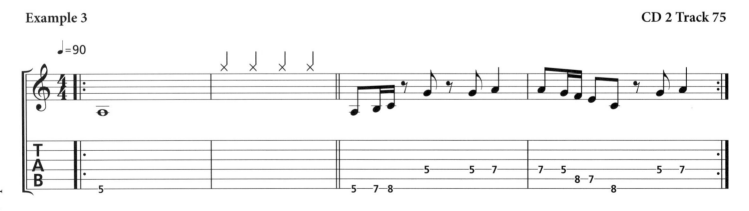

Example 4

CD 2 Track 76

Example 5

CD 2 Track 77

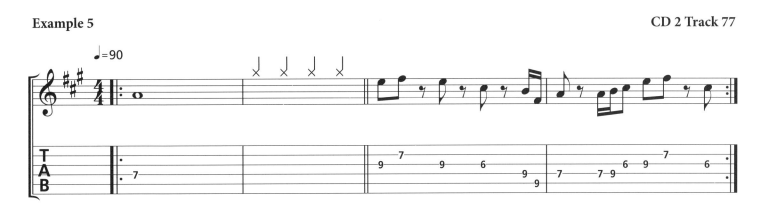

Example 6

CD 2 Track 78

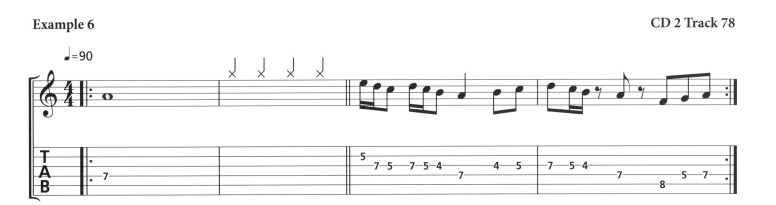

Grade 7 Test 2: Harmonic Recall

The examiner will play you a tonic chord followed by a four-bar chord sequence in the key of A major played to a bass and drum backing. The sequence will use the I, ii, iii, IV, V and vi chords. The ii, iii and vi chords can be either minor or minor [7] chords. You will be asked to play the chord sequence to the bass and drum backing in the rhythm shown in the examples below. This rhythm will be used in all examples of this test given in the exam. You will then be asked to identify the sequence you have played to the examiner, including any chord extensions. You will hear the test twice.

Each time the test is played the sequence is: count-in, tonic, count-in, chords. There will be a short gap for you to practise after you have heard the test for the second time. You will hear the count-in and tonic for the third time followed by a *vocal* count-in and you will then play the chords to the bass and drum backing. You should then name the chord sequence, including the chord type and any extensions.

Example 1   CD 2 Track 79

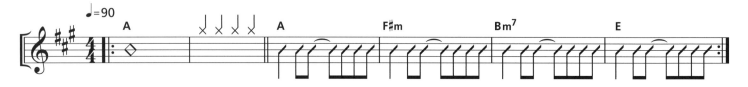

Example 2   CD 2 Track 80

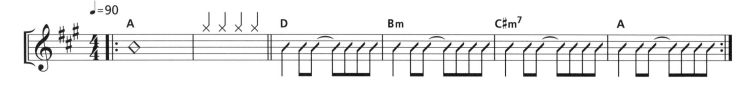

Example 3   CD 2 Track 81

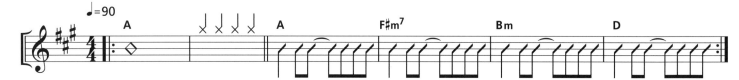

Example 4

CD 2 Track 82

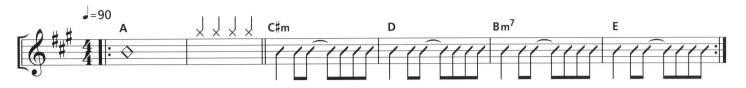

Example 5

CD 2 Track 83

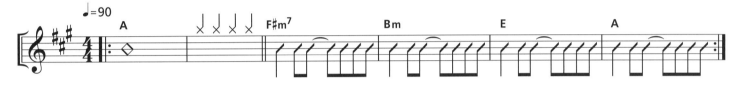

Example 6

CD 2 Track 84

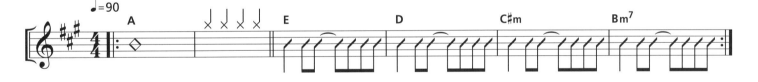

Grade 8 Test 1: Melodic Recall

The examiner will play you a two-bar melody with a bass and drum backing using either the E major pentatonic, F minor pentatonic or B natural minor scale. The first note of the melody will be *either* the root note, third *or* fifth and the first interval will be *either* ascending *or* descending. You will play the melody back on your instrument. You will hear the test twice.

Each time the test is played the sequence is: count-in, root note, count-in, melody. There will be a short gap for you to practise after you have heard the test for the second time. You will hear the count-in and root note for the third time followed by a *vocal* count-in and you will then play the melody to the bass and drum backing.

Example 1   CD 3 Track 1

Example 2   CD 3 Track 2

Example 3   CD 3 Track 3

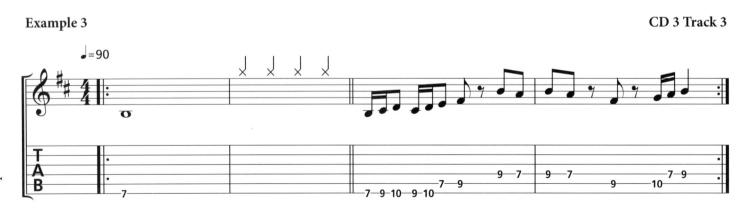

Example 4

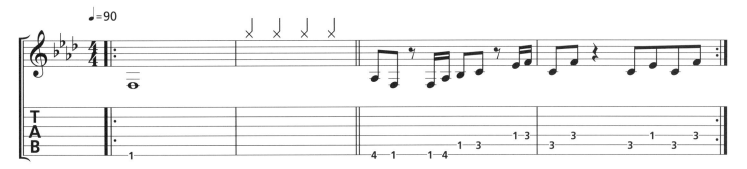

Example 5

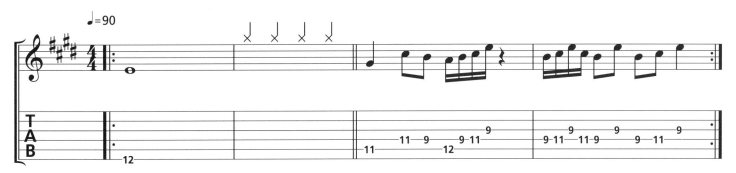

Example 6

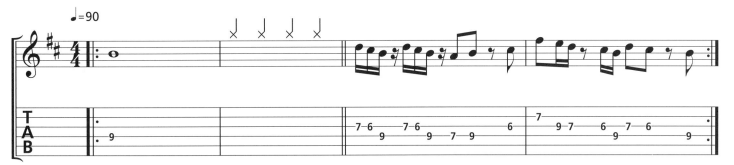

Grade 8 Test 2: Harmonic Recall

The examiner will play you a tonic chord followed by a four-bar chord sequence in the key of E major played to a bass and drum backing. The sequence will use the I, ii, iii, IV, V and vi chords. The I and IV chords can be either major or major[7] chords. You will be asked to play the chord sequence to the bass and drum backing in the rhythm shown in the examples below. This rhythm will be used in all examples of this test given in the exam. You will then be asked to identify the sequence you have played to the examiner, including any chord extensions. You will hear the test twice.

Each time the test is played the sequence is: count-in, tonic, count-in, chords. There will be a short gap for you to practise after you have heard the test for the second time. You will hear the count-in and tonic for the third time followed by a *vocal* count-in and you will then play the chords to the bass and drum backing. You should then name the chords, including any extensions.

Example 1

CD 3 Track 7

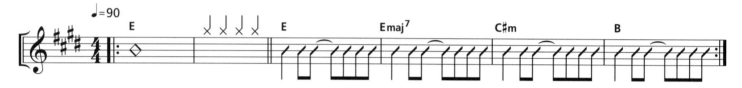

Example 2

CD 3 Track 8

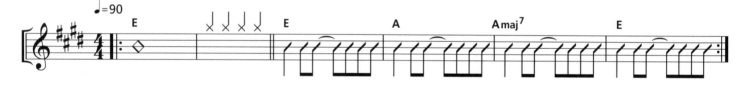

Example 3

CD 3 Track 9

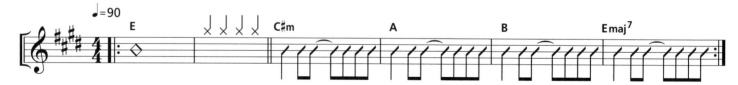

Example 4
CD 3 Track 10

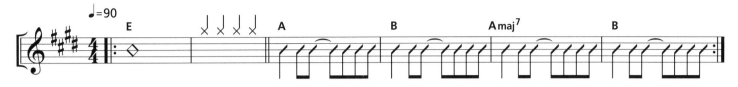

Example 5
CD 3 Track 11

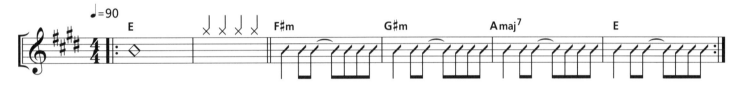

Example 6
CD 3 Track 12

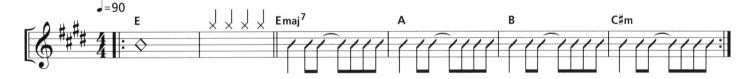

Quick Study Pieces Grade 6

At Grades 6, 7 and 8 you will be asked to prepare and play a short Quick Study Piece (QSP). The QSP is given to candidates during the examination. While preparing for the Technical Exercise section of the exam you will have to select a Stylistic Study from the following three groups: rock/metal, funk or blues/jazz/latin. The choice you make in this section will determine the style of the QSP you are given in the exam. You will be shown the music and played the track with the notated parts played. Any bars that require improvisation will not be demonstrated. You will then have three minutes to study the test. The backing track will be played twice more. You are allowed to practise during the first run through of the backing track, with the notated parts now absent, before playing it to the examiner on the second playing of the backing track. The QSP is in the form of a lead sheet and it is up to you to create your own interpretation of the music in the parts marked for improvisation.

The full technical specifications of the QSPs offered to candidates in the exam can be found in the Guitar *Syllabus Guide* in the summary table on page 35.

Grade 6 Example 1 **CD 3 Tracks 13 & 14**

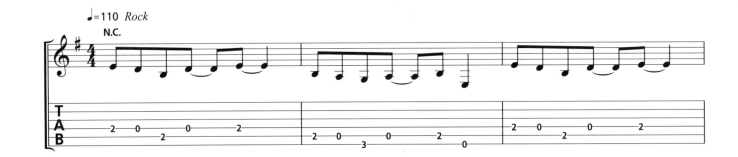

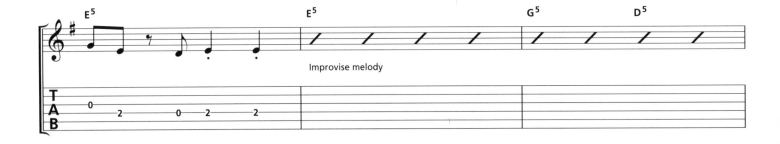

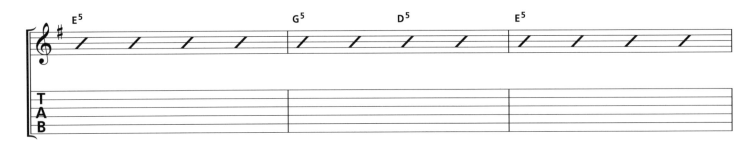

Grade 6 Example 2

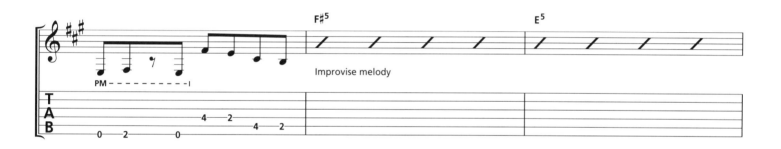

Improvise melody

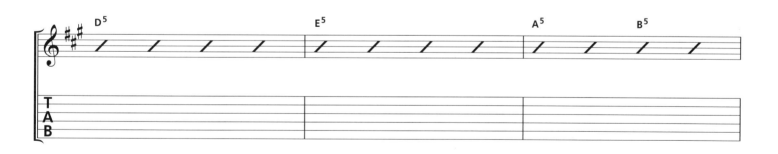

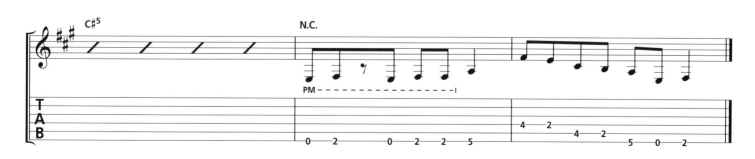

Grade 6 Example 3

CD 3 Tracks 17 & 18

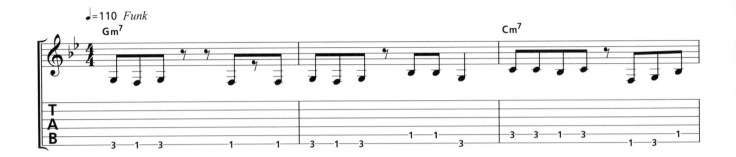

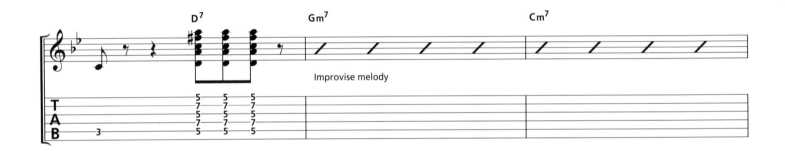

Improvise melody

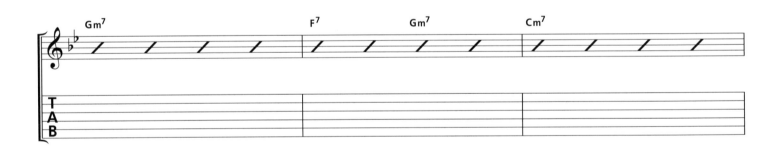

Grade 6 Example 4

CD 3 Tracks 19 & 20

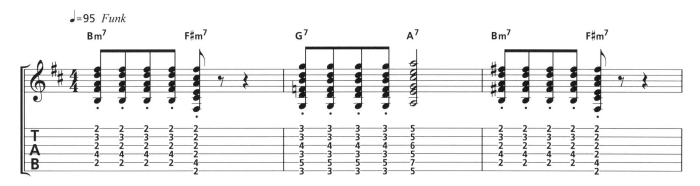

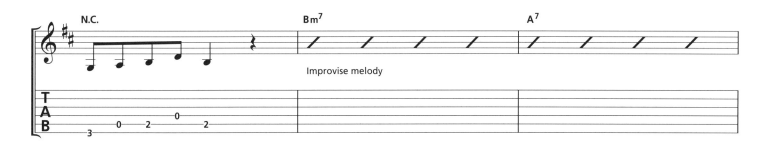

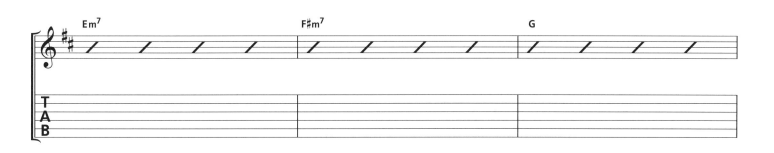

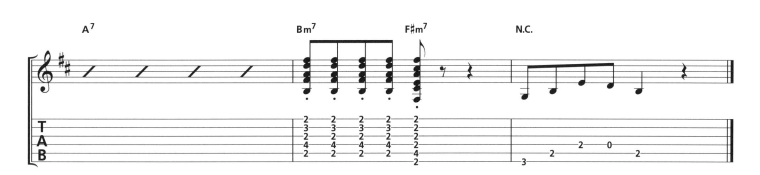

Grade 6 Example 5

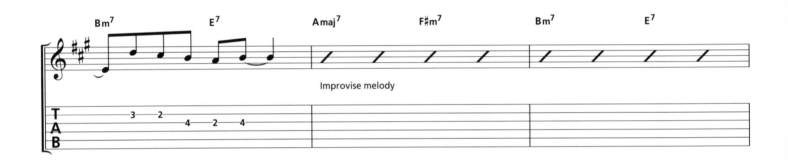

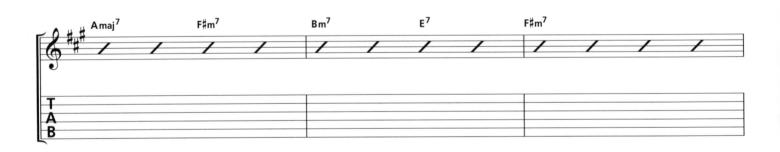

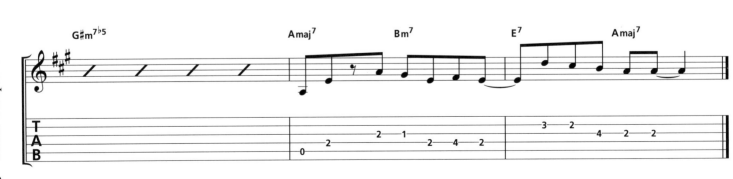

Grade 6 Example 6

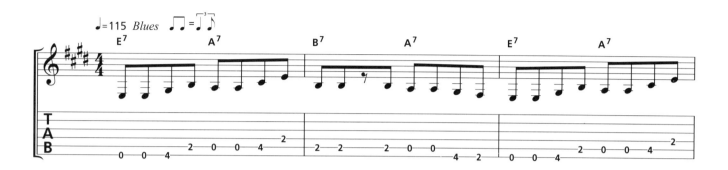

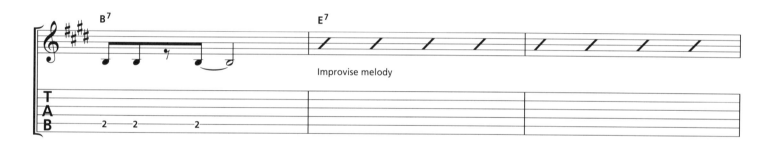

Improvise melody

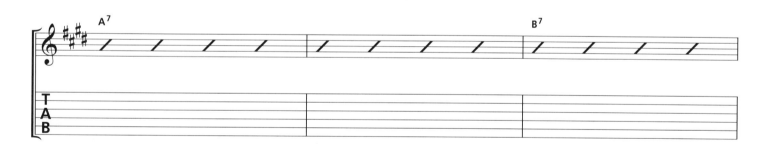

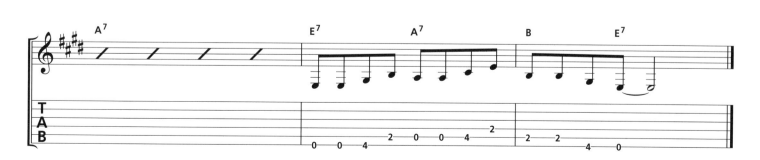

Grade 7 Example 1

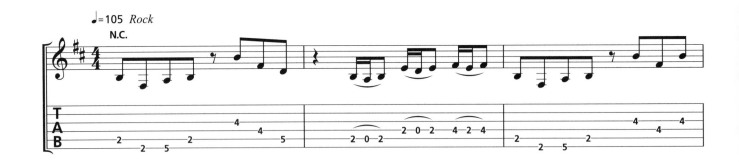

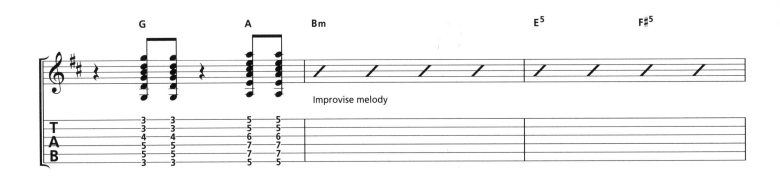

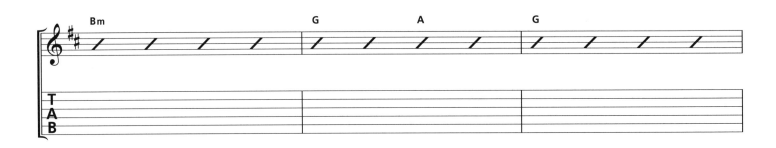

Grade 7 Example 2

CD 3 Tracks 27 & 28

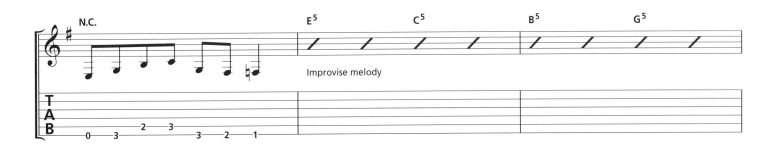

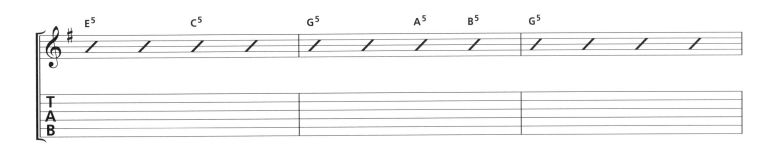

Grade 7 Example 3

CD 3 Tracks 29 & 30

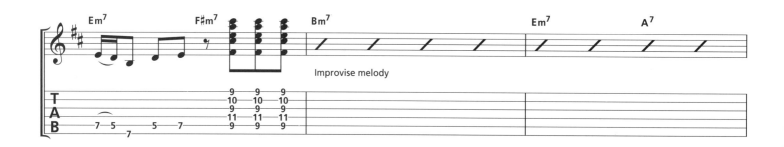

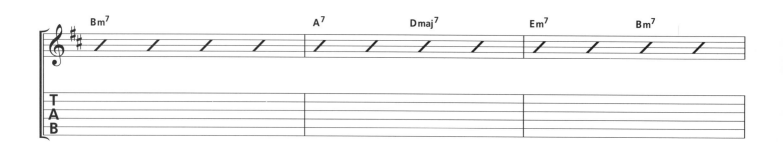

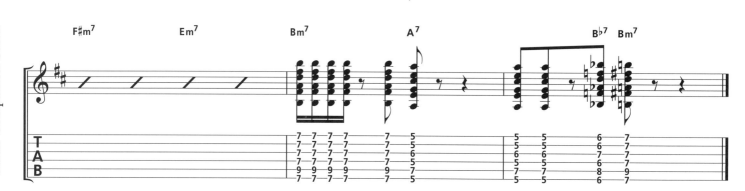

Grade 7 Example 4

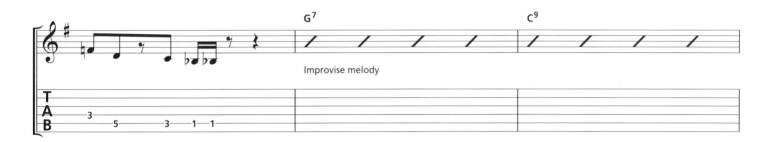

Improvise melody

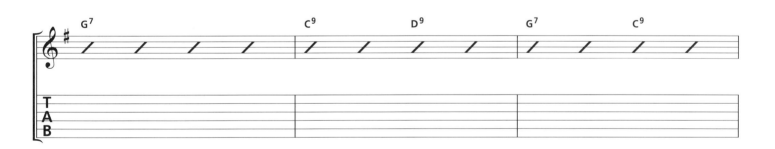

Grade 7 Example 5

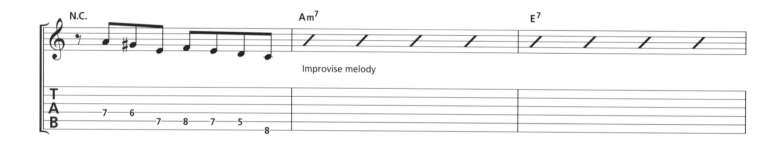

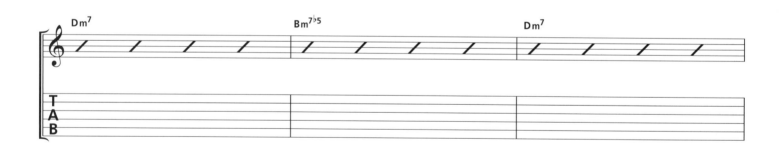

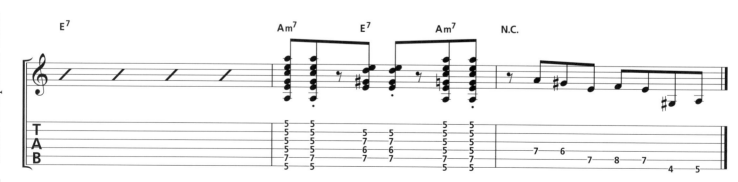

Grade 7 Example 6

CD 3 Tracks 35 & 36

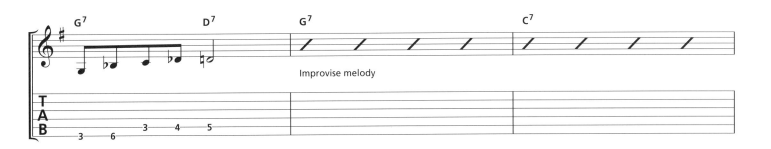

Improvise melody

Quick Study Pieces Grade 8

Grade 8 Example 1

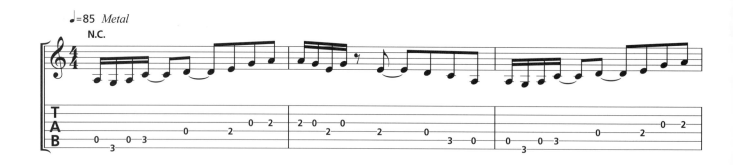

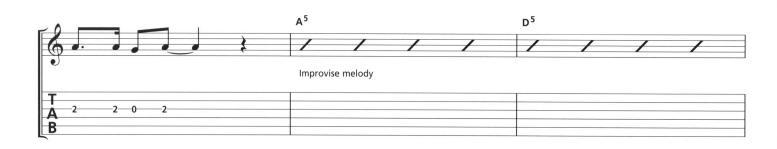

Improvise melody

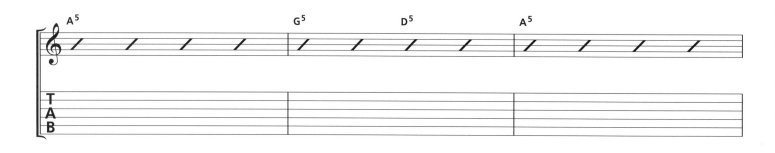

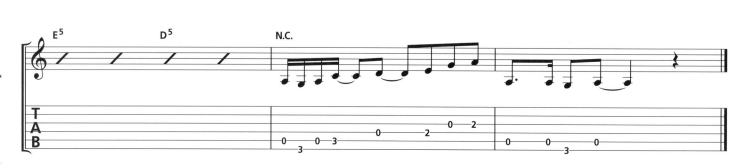

Grade 8 Example 2

CD 3 Tracks 39 & 40

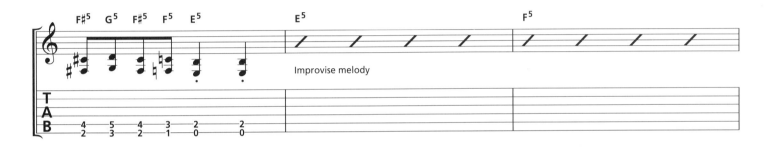

Improvise melody

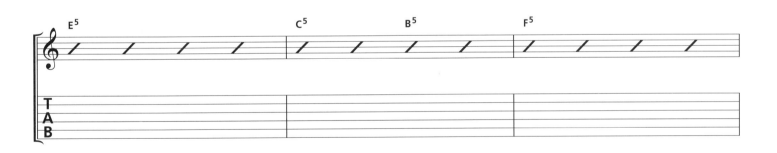

Grade 8 Example 3

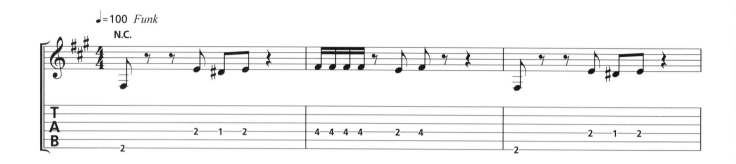

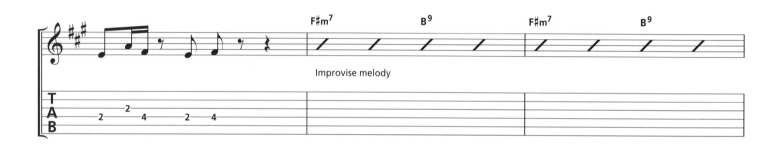

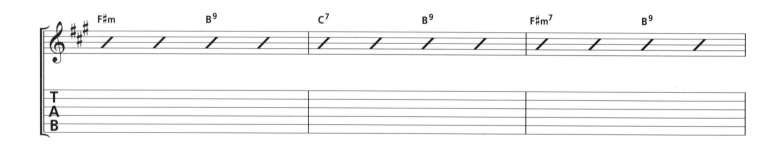

Grade 8 Example 4

CD 3 Tracks 43 & 44

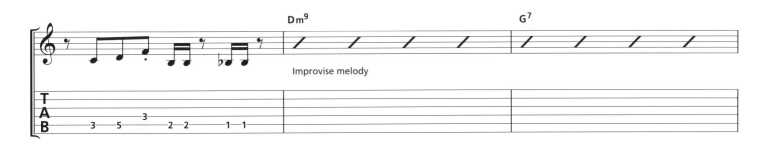

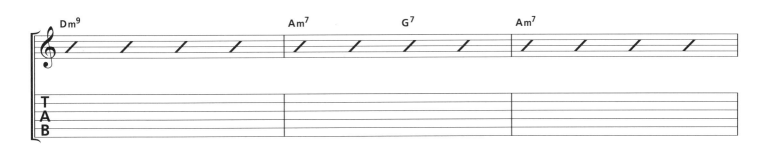

Grade 8 Example 5

CD 3 Tracks 45 & 46

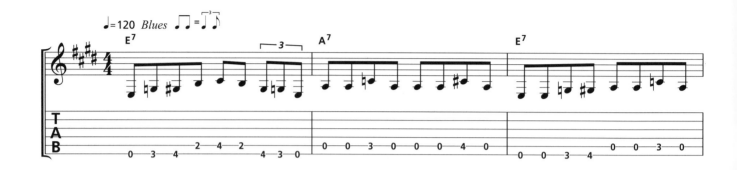

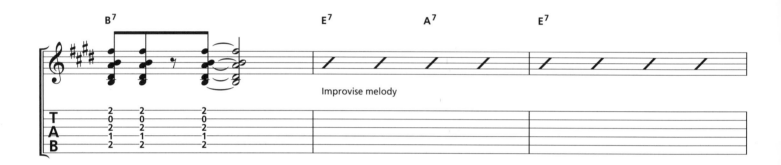

Improvise melody

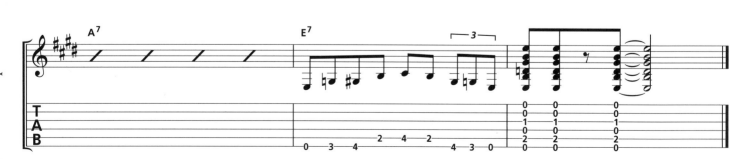

Grade 8 Example 6

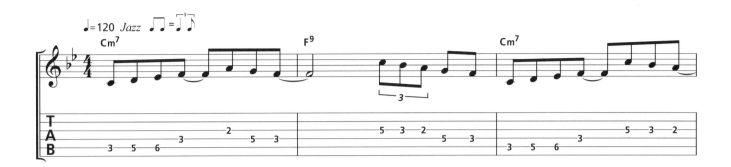

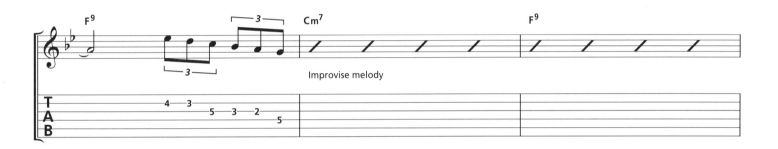

Improvise melody

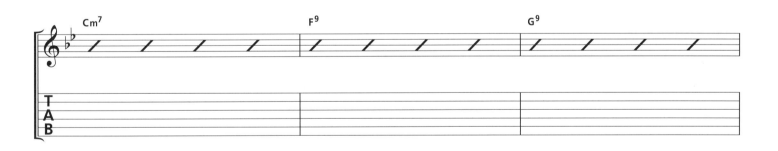

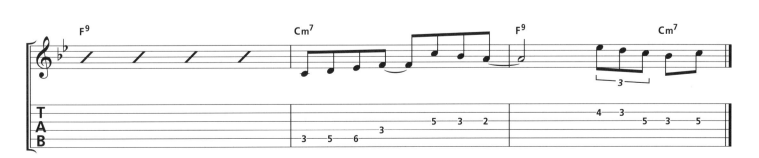

General Musicianship Questions Debut & Grade 1

Each Rockschool grade exam ends with five questions asked by the examiner. The examiner will ask you these questions using a piece played by you as a starting point. Four of the questions will be about general music knowledge and the fifth will be about your instrument.

Here are some sample questions that are typically asked by Rockschool's examiners grade by grade, along with sample answers typically given by candidates.

Debut

The theory questions here refer to the performance piece 'Another Dime' on page 5 of the Guitar Debut candidate book.

  Q. What are the five lines the notes are written on called?
  A. The stave.

  Q. Point to the treble clef for me.
  A. The student identifies the treble clef at the start of the line.

  Q. Point to a note that is a quarter note (crotchet).
  A. The student points to the first note in bar 2.

  Q. What is this note called? [Pointing to the half note in bar 8.]
  A. A half note (minim).

  Q. Where is the nut on your guitar?
  A. The student identifies the nut.

Grade 1

The theory questions here refer to the performance piece 'Just Don't Know', which can be found on page 13 of the Guitar Grade 1 candidate book.

  Q. Point to the time signature for me.
  A. The student identifies the 4/4 at the start of the piece.

  Q. What type of notes are the first two notes in bar 2?
  A. Eighth notes (quavers).

  Q. Point to a whole note in line two.
  A. The student identifies the notes in bar 4.

  Q. What is the difference between a major and minor chord?
  A. Major is happy and minor is sad.

  Q. Name the open strings of your guitar.
  A. E, A, D, G, B and E.

Grade 2

The theory questions here refer to the performance piece 'Ska'd For Life' on page 9 of the Guitar Grade 2 candidate book.

Q. What does 4/4 mean?
A. There are four quarter notes (crotchets) in a bar

Q. What is the pitch name of the first note in bar 3?
A. D.

Q. How long is the rest at the end of bar 4?
A. An eighth note (quaver).

Q. How is a minor chord constructed?
A. Root, minor third, perfect fifth.

Q. Where are the volume and tone controls on your guitar?
A. The student identifies the controls.

Grade 3

The theory questions here refer to the performance piece 'Indecisive' on page 13 of the Guitar Grade 3 candidate book.

Q. What is the value of the last rest in bar 8?
A. A half note (minim).

Q. What is the pitch name of the first two notes in bar 10?
A. G.

Q. What type of notes are these?
A. Eighth notes.

Q. How do you construct a major chord?
A. Root, major third, perfect fifth.

Q. Show me the volume and gain controls on the amp.
A. The student identifies the controls on the amp.

General Musicianship Questions Grades 4 & 5

Grade 4

The theory questions here refer to the performance piece 'Base Jumper' on page 5 of the Guitar Grade 4 candidate book.

Q. Show me the key signature and tell me what it is.
A. The student identifies the sharp and names it as F♯.

Q. What are the thick lines and dots at either end of the first line?
A: Repeat marks, which mean you play the line twice.

Q. How do you construct a dominant^7?
A. Root, major third, perfect fifth and flattened seventh.

Q. What scale could you use in the solo on page two?
A. The G major pentatonic scale for the first half and E minor pentatonic for the second half. The scales have the same notes.

Q. Describe to me the settings you chose for this piece.
A. I went for a high-gain distortion and boosted the bass and treble.

Grade 5

The theory questions here refer to the performance piece 'Geek' on page 5 of the Guitar Grade 5 candidate book.

Q. What does the direction next to the bpm mean?
A. That the eighth notes should be swung.

Q. What type of notes are used in bar 3?
A. Triplet eighth notes.

Q. What does the sign before the note in bar 12 mean?
A. It should be played as C♯.

Q. How is a minor^7 chord constructed?
A. Root, minor third, perfect fifth and minor seventh.

Q. What sort of sound did you use for this piece?
A. I used a modern high-gain distortion with the gain set relatively high.

Grade 6

The theory questions here refer to the performance piece 'That Sounds Like Noise' on page 15 of the Guitar Grade 6 candidate book.

Q. What does D.S. al Coda mean?
A. You go back to the sign and play until the coda sign then play the coda.

Q. What does PH mean in bar 1?
A. Pinched harmonic.

Q. What is the pitch name of the first note?
A. F♯.

Q. What scale could you use for the solo?
A. The F♯ blues scale works well but you can also use the F♯ natural minor scale.

Q. What could you do to vary the sound during the piece?
A. You could add delay for the melody and lead sections.

Grade 7

The theory questions here refer to the performance piece 'The Pants Era' on page 5 of the Guitar Grade 7 candidate book.

Q. What do NH and the diamond shapes round the TAB mean?
A. Natural harmonics. You should place your finger slightly in front of the fret.

Q. What does 11/16 mean?
A. There are 11 16th notes in a bar.

Q. What is the pitch name of the first note of bar 25?
A. E natural.

Q. What scale would you use for the solo other than the minor pentatonic or blues scales?
A. You could use the natural minor with a flattened fifth.

Q. What two key elements make up a typical metal rhythm guitar tone?
A. A modern high-gain distortion and a scooped sound.

Grade 8

The theory questions here refer to the performance piece 'Mind The Gaps' on page 11 of the Guitar Grade 8 candidate book.

    Q. What are the crossed note chords?
    A. Muted chords to achieve a stylistic rhythm.

    Q. What does *mf* mean at the start of the piece?
    A. Moderately loud.

    Q. What does the sign above the note in bar 14 mean?
    A. To be played with vibrato.

    Q. What two scale choices did you make for the solo?
    A. G natural minor for the first half and E♭ lydian for the second half.

    Q. What variations of tone can you use for this piece?
    A. It can be played clean (or with slight distortion) and then with distortion for the solo.